USING THE DRESS COLLECTION AT THE V&A

A HANDBOOK FOR TEACHERS

CONTENTS

INTRODUCTION

The book

This book aims to help secondary school teachers of Art, Textiles and Technology use the V&A's collections of dress to support National Curriculum, GCSE and A-level topics. Some of the ideas can also be adapted for the primary classroom.

Pupils working in the Dress Collection.

The five main chapters each outline projects based on the collections and include related historical information. All the projects depend on a visit to the Museum for their success, and ways of integrating the study of dress while at the V&A to the work done at school are suggested. The historical information supports these particular projects, so you will not find a complete history of dress in this book. There is, however, a visual chronology of dress showing the most important changes in European fashion between the seventeenth and the twentieth centuries. There is also a section on relevant books and other resources.

Although most of the projects focus on the collection of European dress, the V&A offers excellent opportunities for a multicultural approach. Projects involving non-European dress are in the chapters on 'Historical and cross-cultural influences on twentieth-century fashion' and 'Cut and construction'.

Pastel drawing of a detail of a 1977 Yuki evening cloak by an A-level student.

The Museum's collections

The V&A is a museum of art and design, so the clothes have been collected for their aesthetic and stylistic interest as well as their significance in terms of fashion. They are generally examples of outstanding workmanship which would only have been worn by a wealthy minority. There are no children's clothes on display and they are not dealt with in this publication. These can be found at the Bethnal Green Museum of Childhood, a branch of the Victoria and Albert Museum.

The galleries

The main gallery you will need to use is the Dress Collection in Room 40. This is on the ground floor of the Museum, close to the Exhibition Road entrance, which all educational groups are asked to use. It contains examples of European dress from the seventeenth century to the present day, displayed chronologically. Different types of accessories are displayed in separate cases and with the outfits in the main cases. Temporary displays are shown in Cases 59 to 61 and the glass cube case at the entrance to the gallery nearest the Cromwell Road entrance.

Each figure has been mounted so that the garments look as they did when they were worn. Authentically constructed undergarments have been used so that the clothes are correctly supported. The wigs are light-coloured and the faces have pale 'shadow' make-up so that they do not detract from the garments yet give the correct proportions and a balanced appearance for each mannequin.

Close to the Dress Collection are the Nehru Gallery of Indian Art (Room 41), the T.T. Tsui Gallery of Chinese Art (Room 44), the Toshiba Gallery of Japanese Art (Room 45) and the Samsung Gallery of Korean Art (Room 47G). These all contain examples of dress and accessories. The Textile Study Rooms (Rooms 95-101) on the first floor also house examples of East Asian and Middle Eastern dress, and European peasant clothing. There are examples of embroidered sixteenth- and seventeenth-century British garments and accessories in Britain 1500-1715 (Room 53).

Working in the galleries

Dry art materials only are permitted in the galleries unless prior permission of the curatorial department concerned has been gained. Fine rollerball pens are particularly good for making quick sketches of clothes and drawings of closely observed details such as fastenings. Pastels enable pupils to render large areas of colour quickly and are very suitable for conveying folds and pleats, and the shine of silk and satin. Coloured pencils are good for making quick colour notes and the watercolour versions mean that drawings can be worked up back at school.

It is worth bringing a camera to record additional material for pupils to work from back at school. A good technique is to limit each pupil to one or two photos that supplement rather than duplicate their drawings (for example, by choosing a different viewpoint or a detail). The light levels in the Dress Collection are kept low in order to slow down the irreversible fading and physical disintegration of exhibits. You will need a fast film (1,000 ASA is ideal) or a camera with a flash.

From time to time the displays in the galleries are changed and items referred to in this book may be removed.

Sketch of a late 19th-century dress by an A-level student done in fine black pen.

THE CHANGING SHAPE OF FASHION

Clothes can be used to reshape the human figure by constricting or adding to it. Undergarments that do this are sometimes called foundation garments. This is a useful way of thinking of them, as they provide the foundation upon which a fashionable silhouette is built. The dress sculpture project described in this chapter aims to help pupils develop an understanding of the fashionable silhouette in the eighteenth and nineteenth centuries. It focuses on undergarments such as corsets, crinolines and bustles and uses an analysis of their form and construction as the starting point for pupils' own creations.

PROJECT: DRESS SCULPTURE

Activity: to construct a sculpture based on an analysis of eighteenth- and nineteenth-century fashion, in particular highly structured foundation garments such as crinolines. The aim is for students to produce a personal, expressive response based on historical understanding.

Knowledge and understanding: the shape of fashionable clothing in the eighteenth and nineteenth centuries; how underwear relates to outerwear; the materials and construction of foundation garments.

Galleries used: the Dress Collection.

Before the visit

Read out to pupils a list of items of clothing that make up a modern outfit, for example: baseball cap, T-shirt, shorts, socks, trainers. Ask them who would wear this now (the point being that this sort of comfortable clothing is unisex nowadays). In the past, however, clothes for men and women were often sharply differentiated. For women in particular they could also be uncomfortable.

Talk to your pupils about how the fashionable silhouette changed during the eighteenth and nineteenth centuries using the information at the end of this chapter. Discuss some of the gender and health issues that arise - for instance, why has women's clothing so often been restrictive?

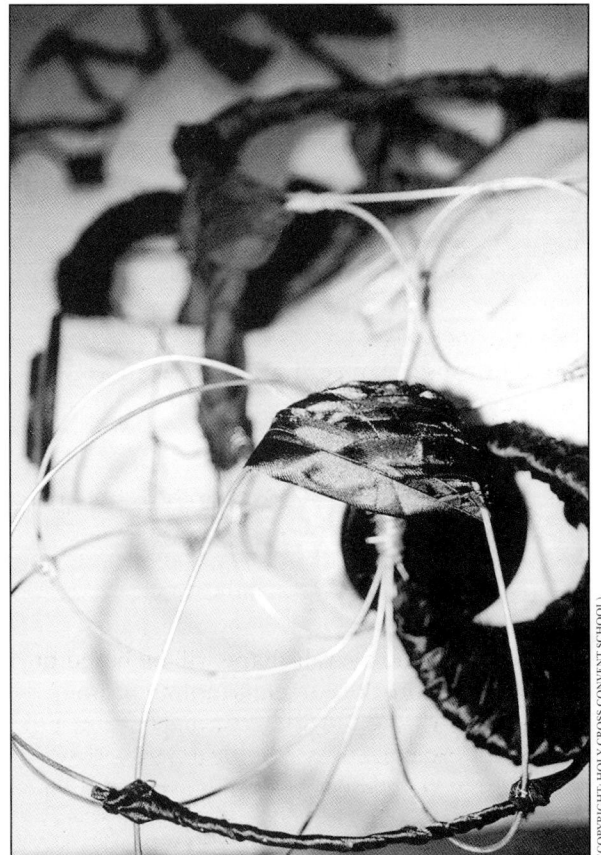

Sculpture based on crinolines, bustles and other elements of 19th-century women's dress by A-level students at Holy Cross Convent School, New Malden.

Think about the sort of silhouette fashionable for men and women today. How is it achieved? Mention padding in particular - shoulder pads, padded bras and so on. You could get pupils to annotate pictures of clothes in magazines to show where they think padding has been used. The use of body-hugging materials such as Lycra, as well as the fashion for sport, healthy eating and keeping fit, could also be discussed.

At the Museum

Start by looking at some of the eighteenth- and nineteenth-century clothes that required foundation garments, like hoop petticoats or bustles. For each garment that you look at talk about the sort of silhouette that is created and ask pupils to think about its advantages and disadvantages. Would it be easy to sit down or walk through a door? Does it show off a large expanse of expensive fabric? Does it exaggerate feminine curves?
Now look at some of the undergarments that helped to create the silhouettes (Cases 30 and 33 have relevant examples). Look in particular at the materials and construction of the corset, crinoline, hoop petticoat and bustle. Discuss the part of the body each undergarment affects.

Your pupils' task is to record those elements that they will use in their sculptures. They will need to draw particularly careful diagrams of the construction of the undergarments. Sketches of trimmings from other garments could be looser, concentrating on form, colour and materials.

Back at school

The task back at school is for pupils to design and make a sculpture based on the garments they have recorded in the Dress Collection. The sculpture will use wire for the main structural elements combined with other materials as appropriate. The overall shape will be based on the form of a bustle, corset, crinoline or hoop petticoat. The way the different materials are joined in the sculpture could also derive from the construction of foundation garments. More decorative elements may be taken from pleats, folds, bows, buttons and other dress trimmings.

Get together an assortment of different materials and tools: a variety of fabrics, paper and card, thin wire, chicken wire, string, wool, beads and buttons, scissors, pliers, wire cutters, craft knives, hole punch, a range of needles,

sellotape, parcel tape. Before starting their sculptures, pupils will need to experiment with different joining techniques using the materials and tools provided. Here are some pointers: when using wire, use thick wire for the main structure and thin wire for joining; winding thin wire round thick wire is a joining technique with a lot of decorative potential; think about punching holes in pieces of card and joining them with string

Master James Ronnie Swinton and Donald, silhouette in cut black paper by August Edouart, 1830.

or wire before attaching them to the main frame; slit and interlock pieces of card; tie fabric and string; thread beads and buttons on to thin wire or thread. You may want to set pupils specific tasks such as 'join two pieces of card with wire' before starting the main piece.

Talk about some of the possibilities for siting a sculpture - for example, it could be floor-based, designed for a wall, or suspended. Your pupils should now be ready to start on their sculpture.

SUPPORTING INFORMATION

The fashionable silhouette in the eighteenth century

At the beginning of the eighteenth century the male silhouette differed greatly from that of today. A typical outfit consisted of a full-skirted knee-length coat, knee breeches, a vest or long waistcoat (which could be sleeved), a linen shirt with frills and linen underdrawers. Lower legs showed and were an important part of the silhouette. Men wore silk stockings and leather shoes with stacked heels of low or medium height. The whole ensemble would have been topped by a shoulder-length full-bottomed wig and a tricorne (three-cornered) hat with an upturned brim.

As the century progressed, the male silhouette slowly changed. By the middle of the century the wig was usually tied back (known as the tye or bag wig). By the end of the century it was out of fashion altogether except for the most formal occasions. Undergarments and knee breeches did not change very much. Coat skirts gradually became less full and the front was cut in a curved line towards the back. Waistcoats became shorter. The upper leg began to show more and by the end of the century breeches fitted better because they were often made of knitted silk. Shoes became low-heeled with pointed toes and were fastened with a detachable buckle and straps or a ribbon on the vamp (the upper front part of a boot or shoe).

Silk suit from the 1760s.

In the early eighteenth century women wore a dress known as a mantua for formal occasions. The mantua was an open-fronted silk or fine wool gown with a train and matching petticoat. The train was worn looped up over the hips to reveal the petticoat. The bodice had loose elbow-length sleeves finished with wide turned-back cuffs. A hoop petticoat and several under-petticoats were worn beneath the outer petticoat.

To give the figure the required shape a corset was worn under the bodice. It was made of linen and stiffened with whale bones inserted between parallel lines of stitching. They fastened with lacing down the back which could be laced tightly to give an upright posture to the torso, lift the bust and constrict the waist. A 'busk' or strip of bone, wood or metal was sometimes incorporated into the front of the stays and served to separate the breasts.

Hair was worn close to the head with a small linen cap which sometimes had lace lappets, streamers that hung either side of a woman's cap. The cap was covered by a hood or hat for outdoor wear.

In the 1730s the 'sack back' dress worn over a hoop petticoat became increasingly fashionable. It remained in fashion until the 1780s. The sack back was made from one or two panels of material pleated into two box pleats at the centre back of the neck band. It flowed down and was incorporated into the fullness of the skirt. It was worn over a matching petticoat as well as a hoop petticoat. The 'nightgown style' or style anglaise had a pleated back. The pleats were stitched flat from the back of the neck to the centre back waist.

Hoop petticoats were usually made of linen with split cane hoops stitched in at intervals and held the skirt of the petticoat and the robe out at the sides. They were at their widest in the 1740s and '50s when they could measure over 1.5m across. Hoop petticoats were worn on formal occasions. As with many fashions, it is hard to say why such a cumbersome outfit was popular. One reason might have been that it displayed the richly embroidered cloth of the skirt which indicated the wearer's wealth.

During the 1770s hair styles became higher, as they were combed over a padded roll or worn over a frame.

Between the 1780s and 1800 a very noticeable change took place in the female silhouette. This

Mantua gown worn over a hoop petticoat, 1744.

can be seen in Case 15. The waistline became higher until it reached the bust. The skirt was reduced in width and hoop petticoats were discarded except at court. In their place crescent-shaped pads were worn at the centre back waist beneath the skirt creating a bustle effect. In the 1790s corsets were lightly boned and usually made of linen. Hair was frizzed or worn in short curls.

The fashionable silhouette in the nineteenth century

By the early nineteenth century men's fashions had also undergone a radical change. The coat still finished in long tails at the back but was cut higher in front. The waist-length, square-cut waistcoat showed beneath it. The lining of the shoulders and upper chest of the coat was sometimes quilted to improve the fit. In the early nineteenth century some dandies wore boned corsets to give them a small waist.

This fashion plate from *Ladies* magazine of 1801 shows the characteristic high waistline of the time.

(E.249-1955)

Gradually men adopted long trousers rather than knee breeches. Trousers became increasingly fashionable in the first quarter of the nineteenth century. At first they were only worn for day and informal dress but by the 1820s they were acceptable for evening wear. Breeches continued to be worn at court.

The tall hat from the late eighteenth century was still worn and developed into the top hat which was worn for day and formal dress throughout the nineteenth century. Hair was carefully styled into a windswept look or worn short and curled.

During the second half of the nineteenth century men retained the white waistcoat and black tail-coat and trousers of the early nineteenth century for evening wear. For day wear they wore a frock coat with straight trousers, a short waistcoat and a shirt with a high stiff collar. The single- or double-breasted frock coat fitted quite closely to the torso and had a waist seam. The skirts were straight and finished at mid-thigh or below. The front of the coat was square cut. Hair was still styled but by the late nineteenth century it was short and cut close to the head. Many men had beards and moustaches.

As the nineteenth century progressed women's dress gradually revealed the actual form of the body. In the 1820s and '30s the

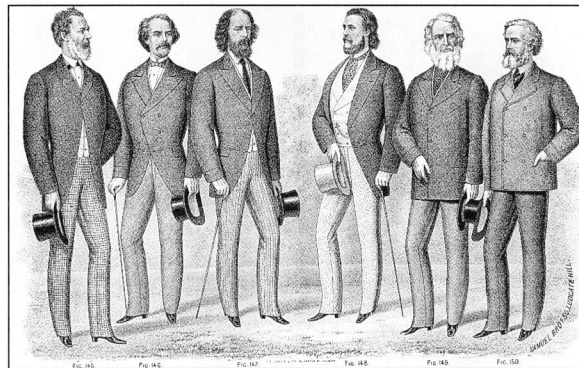

(LIBRARY)

English fashions for men from the 1868 catalogue of Samuel Brothers, a London firm making mass-produced clothes.

From left to right are a 'professional Oxonian suit', a 'double-breasted morning suit', a 'Cambridge suit', a 'dress Oxonian' suit, a 'negligee suit' and a 'yachting suit'.

waistline deepened, returning to its natural position. As the natural waist returned the bodice required a tighter fit and in contrast the skirt became fuller and bell-shaped. There were several different sleeve styles but short puffed sleeves were generally worn for evening and long sleeves for day. Corsets continued to be worn.

(948 D)

Monstrosities of 1822 by George Cruikshank. This etching caricatures the fashionable male silhouette of the time - padded shoulders and chest and a waist nipped in with a corset.

These were lightly-boned and quilted, with a deep busk. Several layers of petticoats with frilled hems, sometimes of horsehair, were worn to support the full skirts. Some petticoats of the 1840s were feather-quilted. Later examples of the 1850s and '60s were made of 'crin' and steel hoops. The term 'crinoline' is derived from the French word *crin*, which means horsehair.

Bonnets or hats were worn outdoors and linen caps indoors. During the 1820s hair styles became very elaborate with raised top knots and the crowns of bonnets or hats were designed to accommodate them. By the middle of the century, by contrast, hairstyles had become smooth with a central parting finished with ringlets on either side of the face and a small bun at the back or simply swept back from the face to a chignon (a mass of hair arranged on a pad at the back of the head and held in place with a net or snood). Bonnets and hats continued to be worn until the 1860s when small, elegant styles appeared which simply perched on top of the head. Even smaller hats appeared in the 1870s when hairstyles rose in the form of elaborate chignons. In the 1880s and '90s hairstyles remained 'up' but did not retain the heights or bulk of the 1870s styles. Small hats decorated with birds and feathers and artificial flowers were fashionable.

In the 1860s the skirt was very full and worn over a cage crinoline, a petticoat supported by a frame of steel hoops that held it away from the legs. A boned corset was worn over a chemise. Large shawls were sometimes worn indoors or outdoors instead of a coat or cloak.

The 1870s to '80s introduced styles that revealed the natural silhouette. A popular style was the 'princess line' dress, which was made without a waist seam to reveal the figure. Skirts fitted tightly and required streamlined all-in-one underwear (combinations). Corsets became longer and were more rigidly boned. The busk, known as the spoon busk because of its shape, extended to the stomach. Sleeves were tight. In the 1880s a bustle pad, or a tier of stiffened horsehair or fabric frills, was introduced. After 1887-88 the bustle went out of fashion. Hair was curled on top and taken into a bun at the back. Often a ringlet was brought forward over the shoulder as a finishing touch.

By the 1880s an élite group of women began to adopt simpler and easier styles that were known as 'artistic' dress. Artistic dress was cut much more loosely than conventional attire and did not require restrictive corsetry to be worn.

During the last years of the nineteenth century it was fashionable for women's hair to be arranged on the top of the head in a bun and puffed out around the face. A large-brimmed hat would be fastened on with hat pins unless a simpler, smaller hat, such as the straw boater, was required for informal dress. The skirt was

Dress with a pattern that complements the shape created by the cage crinoline worn underneath it, 1858-60.

(T.702-1913)

Front view of a sateen and leather corset, 1883. The leather panel on either side of the opening contains a 'spoon busk' made of whalebone which was intended to exert an equalized and non-harmful pressure on the stomach.

(T.84-1980)

Photograph of William Morris' daughter May, wearing 'artistic' dress, Frederick Hollyer, 1884.

(PH.7816-1938)

floor length with a slight train. The waist remained small and a corset which either laced up or fastened with clips was generally worn. A small pad was worn at the back of the waist to support the skirt. In the 1890s the top of the sleeves were sometimes puffed into an enormous 'leg of mutton' shape which required lightweight stiffening or padding. The neckline for day wear was very high featuring a stand-up collar in a lightweight fabric which was boned or wired around the edge to hold it up under the chin. Women adopted a simple and rather masculine-looking shirt, jacket and skirt for day wear.

Towards the end of the nineteenth century the rate at which the fashionable silhouette changed quickened. The increasing popularity of paper patterns and the growth of women's fashion periodicals encouraged home dress-making during the second half of the nineteenth century. The withdrawal of the paper tax in the middle of the nineteenth century had stimulated the growth of publications, especially magazines aimed at women. It was during this period that magazines introduced paper patterns.

By the twentieth century the pace of change in the fashionable silhouette became ever more rapid as the expanding fashion industry, in conjunction with the media, became more effective at stimulating demand for a constant flow of new styles.

HISTORICAL AND CROSS-CULTURAL INFLUENCES ON TWENTIETH-CENTURY FASHION

Among the many factors that have contributed to fashion this century, historical and cross-cultural influences are among those that can easily be studied at the V&A.

The project on fashion design described below gives pupils an opportunity to use the V&A's collections in the way that professional designers do. Paul Poiret and Vivienne Westwood are just two of the many designers who have used the V&A to get ideas for their designs. Pupils will start by looking at examples of the way designers have used historical and non-European dress in their work. They will make a record of a garment in the Museum's collections and feed this into an original design of their own back at school.

PROJECT: FASHION DESIGN

Activity: to design a garment based on an item in the V&A's collections of European and non-European dress and produce either a garment that is stylistically similar or a collage.

Knowledge and understanding: the ways in which twentieth-century fashion designers have used historical sources and ideas from different cultures in their designs.

Galleries to be used: the Dress Collection; the Nehru Gallery of Indian Art (Room 41); the T.T. Tsui Gallery of Chinese Art (Room 44); the Toshiba Gallery of Japanese Art (Room 45); the Samsung Gallery of Korean Art (Room 47G)

(COPYRIGHT TOLWORTH GIRLS' SCHOOL)

Waistcoat with an embroidered motif based on flowers in Indian chintz, by an A-level student at Tolworth Girls' School, Surbiton.

Before the visit

If you intend your pupils to design and make a garment they should have previous experience of making clothes from commercial patterns, and be familiar with basic dress-making skills. Before the visit to the V&A discuss the work of some contemporary designers such as Vivienne Westwood, Issey Miyake and Christian Lacroix. These designers all make use of aspects of historical dress and/or ideas from many different cultures in their designs. The supporting information discusses examples of their work.

If you want pupils to make a collage, they will need to do some large-scale life-drawings before the visit. This will help pupils with proportions when they are drawing clothes in the Dress Collection. Their final designs can be done as a collage on top of the life drawings.

At the Museum

In the Dress Collection discuss with pupils a variety of twentieth-century garments that reveal evidence of historical and non-European design sources. When you make a preliminary visit use the information at the end of this chapter to help you select the things you want to talk about. Five or six outfits ought to be enough. Here are some suggestions: 'Delphos' dress and kimono style jacket by Mariano Fortuny in Case 43; the New Look suit, 'Bar', by Christian Dior, Case 50; single-breasted man's 'Edwardian' suit by Carr, Sonn and Woor of Cambridge in Case 50; the dress by Bill Gibb in Case 54; Pirate outfit by Vivienne Westwood, Case 54; 'Rhythm Pleats' dress by Issey Miyake, Case 54. Follow this by looking at some of the sources that have influenced their design, both in the earlier sections of the Dress Collection and in the nearby galleries of Indian, Chinese and Japanese art.

Your pupils' task is to select a garment they particularly like in the Dress Collection or in one of the non-European galleries. Limit the time available for choosing to about 15 minutes. Pupils will then record their chosen garments through drawings, notes and photographs, ensuring that they get information about cut, shape, colour, decoration, fabric, texture, fastenings and any interesting design details. You will want to have a range of dry art materials available.

You may want to use the study guide opposite to guide your pupils' research. The questions provide a framework that will help pupils record a garment as fully as possible.

Back at school

Pupils will develop their designs, incorporating elements of the item of clothing they recorded. If you are going to make up actual garments, unless you and your pupils have experience of pattern-cutting, you may want to use commercial patterns similar to the designs and modify them as required.

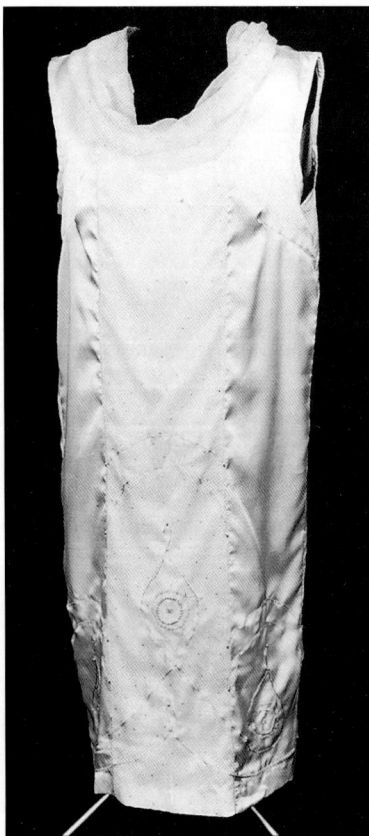

Dress based on a 1920s tubular dress by a GCSE student at Kingswinford School, West Midlands.

(COPYRIGHT: KINGSWINFORD SCHOOL)

SUPPORTING INFORMATION

Some historical and cross-cultural sources for twentieth-century fashion

Throughout the twentieth century cross-cultural and historical influences have exerted a profound impact upon fashion design. The styles, designs and materials of other times and cultures have become more accessible to designers at first hand as improved travel and communications enable continents to be crossed with ease. With developments in photographic and printing techniques, they have also been able to glean ideas from secondary sources such as lavishly illustrated books, magazines and journals. Certainly since the 1950s European designers need only to look around them to see a rich variety of clothing from all corners of the world.

Of the early years of the twentieth century it is the clothes designed by Paul Poiret and Mariano Fortuny that reveal the richest evidence of historical and multicultural sources. Paul Poiret was much influenced by the art and design of the Middle East and India. In about 1910 he visited the V&A to study Indian turbans and, just weeks later, his haute couture adaptations were on sale in Paris. For his 'Thousand and Second Night' fancy dress ball of 1911, Poiret dressed his wife in a wired lampshade tunic over harem trousers. This was to provide the inspiration for his more restrained 'Sorbet' ensemble of 1912, an example of which is on display in Case 43.

Sketch by an A-level student of 'Sorbet', designed by Paul Poiret in 1912.

DRESS *STUDY* GUIDE

Write your answers and make sketches on a separate piece of paper.

SHAPE

What type of garment is it?

Make quick sketches of the whole garment
(showing front, back and side views if possible).

How does the garment fit the figure?

Does it fit differently at different points?

Are there any darts, pleats or gathers? Mark them on your sketches.

Is it belted?

Do you think any special undergarments would be needed?

MATERIALS

What material is the garment made from?

What colour is the garment?

Is the fabric patterned?

Does it have an interesting texture?

Do a colour drawing of a section including colour, pattern and texture.

What fastenings and trimmings are there? Make sketches.

What are they made of?

THE SOCIAL CONTEXT

On what sort of occasion do you think the garment would have been worn?

Clothes can say a lot about the self-image and status of the wearer -
what sort of person might have worn this garment?

What would it have said about them?

YOUR OPINION

Would you like to wear the garment?

Would it be comfortable?

Would you have to be careful when wearing it?

Could you put it on yourself or would you need help?

FINAL FACTS

What date was it made?

Where was it made?

Do you know who designed it?

Fortuny was inspired by a variety of cultures and historical periods and freely combined East Asian, Coptic Egyptian, North African, Classical Greek and Renaissance sources. His finely pleated, black 'Delphos' dress derives from a statue of a charioteer found in Delphi. The form of jacket worn with it was said by Fortuny to be suggested by the kimono. When laid out flat the jacket is rectangular in shape; the side seams stop short of the shoulders to create the arm holes. It is made from silk velvet, widely considered to be the most noble of Renaissance fabrics. The small naturalistic design, printed with metallic pigments, was also inspired by sixteenth-century Italian textiles.

'Delphos' dress and evening jacket, Mariano Fortuny, c.1920.

During the early 1920s, couture houses embellished evening dresses with embroidered and beaded decoration in Chinese style or like that in Russian peasant tradition. In direct contrast, fashion in the 1930s saw a move towards a more feminine silhouette, with bias-cut clothes in smooth fabrics emphasizing the natural contours of the body.

The late 1930s witnessed a move away from this body-skimming line in favour of historically inspired corsetted dresses with crinolines and bustles for evening wear. This trend can be seen in Molyneux's pale-pink ribbed-silk evening dress of 1939 which has a double-tiered full skirt held out by four bone hoops. A less extreme example of the vogue for period revivalism can be seen in Elsa Schiaparelli's black, satin-backed rayon marocain evening suit of 1938. (Marocain is a heavy crêpe fabric.) This ensemble's leg-of-mutton sleeves, tight bodice with nipped-in waist, use of marocain fabric and ostrich-feather-plumed hat were all features of late nineteenth-century fashion. However, the rayon fibre and the bold plastic 'Lightning' zip from ICI were progressive and characteristic Schiaparelli touches.

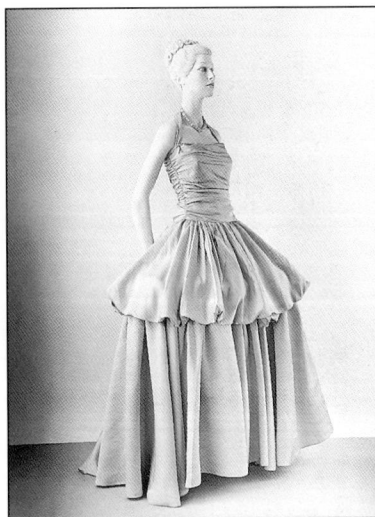

Evening dress, Edward Molyneux, 1939.

During the Second World War clothing was subject to quantitative and design restrictions that aimed to conserve scarce resources while also retaining some element of style. These clothes, produced within the Utility scheme in Britain and under L85 regulations in America, do not reveal any marked historical or cross-cultural influences.

In 1947 Christian Dior launched his 'New Look' collection which, in direct contrast to wartime clothing, revelled in the unashamed luxury and corsetted styles of the late nineteenth century. His 'Bar' suit from the spring of 1947 in cream silk tussore and fine black wool crêpe is made to fit a tiny 45.5cm corsetted waist and exploits just under 7.5m of fabric in the skirt alone. Although a minority of women considered it anachronistic, the New Look was a resounding success among the war-weary population, for whom it evoked the stability of a previous era and embodied hopes for a better future. The promotion of an exaggeratedly feminine figure was in keeping with the prevalent view that women should give up the paid employment they had undertaken as part of the war effort and return to the home.

New Look suit, 'Bar', Christian Dior, 1947; this example photographed by Willy Maywald in Paris is almost identical to the one on display in the Dress Collection in Case 50.

By 1950 revivalist styles, so evident in women's fashions, also invaded the most exclusive levels of menswear. The smart single-breasted grey wool 'Edwardian' suit from 1951 - bowler hat, fitted jacket and tapered trousers worn with waisted overcoat and velvet collar - reveals this brief trend. This was to become the source for Teddy boy street styles.

From 1960 to about 1967 fashion celebrated modernity and scientific progress. However, in spite of the use of new materials and space age imagery, the short shift shape of womenswear dominant at this time can be traced back to the 1920s. The surface patterning of this period also had historical sources: the swirling forms of psychedelia had roots in turn of the century art nouveau designs.

By the late 1960s optimism turned to concern as rising inflation, unemployment and environmental issues came to the fore. Designers began

(T.222 TO C-1974)

This detail of a 1972 Renaissance evening outfit by Bill Gibb shows his interest in historical dress.

to look to nations of the so-called 'Third World' for inspiration and nostalgically turned to the past, especially the 1930s and '40s, for stylistic guidance. In the luxurious world of high fashion Bill Gibb became famous for his clothes embellished with appliqué and embroidered designs. A full-skirted 1972 dress with matching turban reflects the mood for clothing with a gentle ethnic influence. It is made of patchworked cotton fabrics designed by Susan Collier and Sarah Campbell for Liberty and has applied leather thongs and streamers.

After the hard imagery of late 1970s punk, Vivienne Westwood created her nostalgic, neo-romantic Pirate Collection. The pirate outfit, consisting of tunic top and sash, waistcoat, jacket and trousers with bicorne (two-cornered) hat and heavy boots from 1980 draws on a variety of historical and cultural sources. For example, the long slits in the arms of the jacket refer to the sixteenth- and seventeenth-century fashion for slashed fabric.

The Japanese designer, Issey Miyake, shows an interesting combination of influences in the 1990 dress 'Rhythm Pleats'. The fine pleating is reminiscent of Fortuny. However, the choice of fabric (a hi-tech polyester and linen mix which is baked in an oven to set the pleats) means that the garment forms angular, sculptural shapes on the body, rather than clinging to it as the Fortuny does. The lack of concern with revealing the body and the simplicity of the basic shape – when laid out flat the dress forms a rectangle – are evidence of East Asian traditions.

In the 1990s fashion design has become increasingly diverse. Christian Lacroix's bridal gown from 1993 combines ideas from the seventeenth-century Spain of Velazquez's 'Las Meninas' with gypsy sources. A Paul Smith suit mixes flamboyant patchwork fabrics from Afghanistan with 1950s tailoring, while a Helen Storey ensemble reveals modern street and sportswear influences mixed with ethnic-inspired embroidered decoration. It uses modern stretchy Lycra fabrics as well as leather.

(T.354 TO C-1974)

Pirate outfit, Vivienne Westwood, 1980.

CUT AND CONSTRUCTION

Two projects are described in this chapter. The one on T-shaped garments offers a chance to explore the Museum's collections of East Asian dress. The project on skirts considers how an analysis of the often complex garments in the Dress Collection can be used to select and modify a commercially available skirt pattern.

The projects will be of particular use to those teachers who have not previously done any dressmaking with their pupils, or as a first project for pupils just starting an examination course.

PROJECT: T-SHAPED GARMENTS

Activity: to design and make a T-shaped garment based on traditional East Asian dress.

Knowledge and understanding: the cut and construction of T-shaped garments from China, Japan and Korea.

Galleries used: the T.T. Tsui Gallery of Chinese Art (Room 44); the Toshiba Gallery of Japanese Art (Room 45); the Samsung Gallery of Korean Art (Room 47G).

(COPYRIGHT: THE TIFFIN GIRLS' SCHOOL)

Display of T-shaped garments with preparatory work by Year 10 pupils at The Tiffin Girls' School, Kingston-upon-Thames.

Before the visit

Get together some examples of the most familiar western T-shaped garment, the T-shirt, made of different materials. Ask pupils to model the T-shirts and look at how the shape behaves in different fabrics. Look too at any other differences in design such as the neckline and the proportions. Drawing the models wearing T-shirts will reinforce the discussion. Tell pupils to look particularly closely at the way the fabric folds and wrinkles on the body.

The finish of simple garments like T-shirts is crucial to their success – direct pupils to pay attention to the way the neck, sleeves, seams and hem are finished on the examples you have brought in. Has a stretchy band been used at the neck? Has double-stitching been used? This sort of observation will be helpful to pupils when they make their own T-shaped garment.

At the Museum

On a preliminary visit you should identify one or two T-shaped garments each from China, Japan and Korea that you would like to talk about. Discuss these with your pupils at the Museum. Concentrate on the cut, fabric and finish. Use the information on East Asian dress at the end of this section to help you point out aspects of the construction that pupils may not otherwise notice. You will find that by comparing garments that are basically similar in cut, your pupils will start to become aware of differences in detail.

Pupils might make drawings of one or two of the garments, concentrating on the overall shape, the position of seams, and fastenings. They should also do drawings of decorative motifs. Finish the session by taking them to the Dress Collection to look at European clothes that may have been influenced by East Asian cut and construction. There is an eighteenth-century man's brocaded silk nightgown (a T-shaped garment worn indoors as informal dress over breeches and a waistcoat) in Case 4 which shows the influence of the kimono. Two further items to look at are a jacket by Mariano Fortuny (Case 43), and a dress by Issey Miyake (Case 54). They are similar to some types of East Asian dress in that they are both very simple rectangular shapes when laid out flat. You can find out more information about them in the chapter on 'Historical and cross-cultural influences on twentieth-century fashion' pp.9-13.

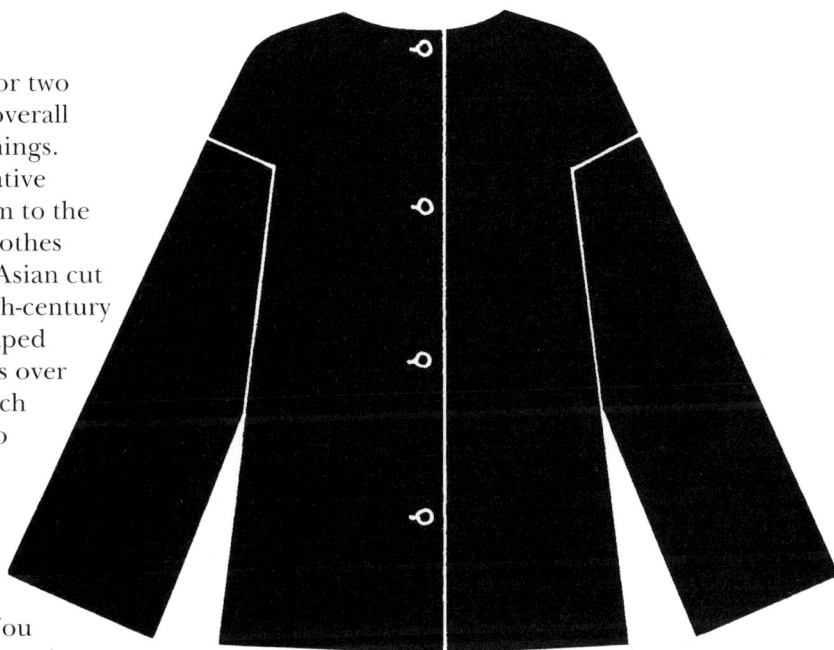

Back at school

Pupils will develop a design based on the T-shaped garments they saw at the Museum. Final sketches will be developed into a paper pattern using the diagrams that follow. You will have to help pupils adapt the basic design described here so that they can incorporate individual elements. They will each need two or three pieces of pattern paper, a tape measure and a metre rule. A pattern-cutting wheel is optional. A supply of cheap fabric will be needed to make up trial versions of the garments.

Before cutting out the final version of their garments pupils might adapt one of their drawings of motifs so that it can be block or screen-printed on to the fabric they are going to use. Alternatively one or two motifs could be embroidered on to the garment (pupils will get better results if they support the fabric with an embroidery frame) or drawn on with fabric pens or crayons. This should be done after the fabric has been cut out but before sewing so that if it goes wrong pupils will not have wasted too much time and energy.

A simple, symmetrical T-shaped garment like the one shown here can be made from a pattern based on measurements taken from the body. Pupils should work in pairs, each pupil making a paper pattern of his or her own.

The first step is to draw a rectangle in the middle of a large piece of pattern paper with a sharp pencil. The width is the measurement from shoulder point to shoulder point across the back (using the bony bit at the top of the arm as the measuring point). The length is taken first from the nape of the neck to the waist, which is marked ('w' on the diagram), then extended to the desired length of the garment. Pupils should work from the designs they developed from drawings done at the Museum.

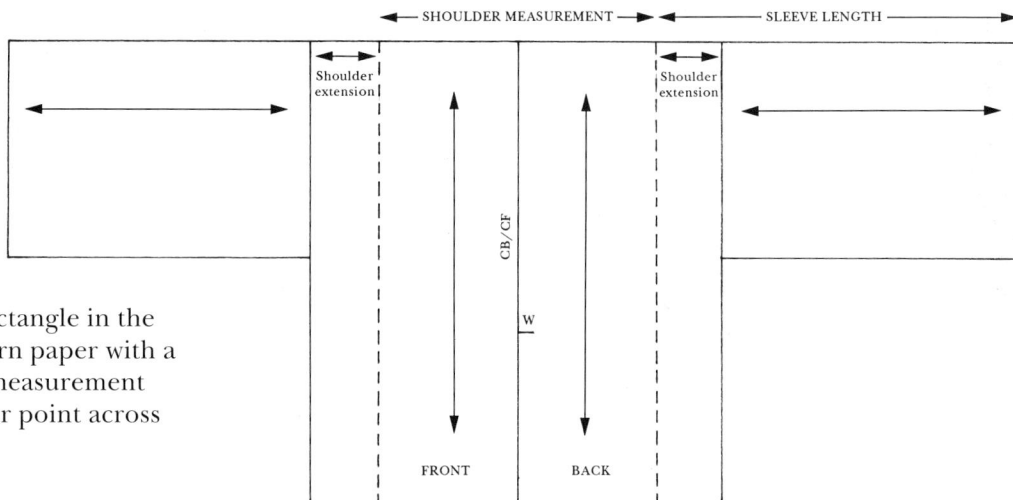

A mark is made half-way across the width at the top and the bottom and the two points are joined with a straight line. This line is the centre front/centre back line ('CF/CB' on diagram). On either side another parallel line is drawn along part of the length, with an arrow at either end. This is the straight grain line. When the pattern is made up it is placed on the straight grain of the fabric, parallel to the selvedge. The right half of the rectangle will be developed into a pattern for the back of the garment, the left half will be used for the front.

The shoulder line should be extended evenly on either side of top of the rectangle according to pupils' designs (between 10cm and 20cm at each side). The same measurements are made at the base of the rectangle and the top and bottom are joined together.

Pupils should use their designs to decide on the length and width of the sleeves. For the length, they should take a measurement from the shoulder to the point where they want the sleeves to finish (wrist, elbow, etc.). The amount that was added previously as a shoulder extension is subtracted to arrive at the sleeve length. When they are deciding on the width of the sleeves pupils should bear in mind that very narrow sleeves are difficult to do on this type of garment (20cm to 30cm is about right). The sleeve width is marked on the back and front

bring the front neckline down in a diagonal line to the hem, which would make it similar to the kimono and the Korean court robe. It would allow the finished garment to wrap over and be secured with a tie or belt.

If pupils want to flare the body of the garment, like the Chinese dragon robe or the Korean court robe, they should draw a couple of straight vertical lines about half-way between the sleeve extension point and the neck point. This is done on both the front and the back pattern piece. They should cut the inner line with

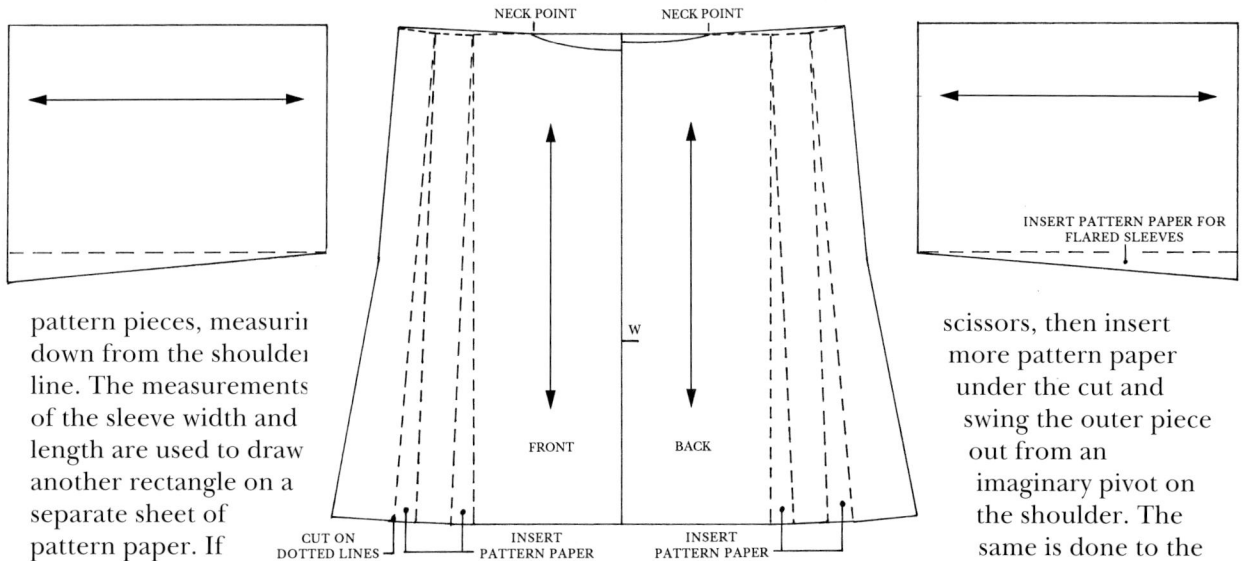

pattern pieces, measuring down from the shoulder line. The measurements of the sleeve width and length are used to draw another rectangle on a separate sheet of pattern paper. If pupils have looked at Chinese dragon robes they may want to taper the sleeve and so will need to cut away pattern paper. They may even want to attempt a separate cuff in the Chinese 'horsehoof' style (see the illustration showing the layout of pattern pieces for a dragon robe on p.20). Flares can be achieved by adding pattern paper.

The next stage is to put in the neckline. The width is calculated by measuring across the base of the neck between the points where the sides of the neck hit the collarbone - the front neck points. This should come to about 24cm. The width is marked on the shoulder line, using the centre front/centre back line as a mid point. This is the side of the neckline.

On the left-hand (i.e. front) side of the centre front/centre back line pupils should make a mark approximately 3cm down from the top, depending on their designs. On the right-hand (i.e. back) side they should make a mark about 1cm down from the top, again depending on their designs. Each mark is then joined up with the correct side of the neckline. If this is done with a loose, broken line pupils will find they get a smoother curve. The line can be joined up later. Remember, the back of the neckline is normally higher than the front. If pupils are making fairly wide garments they may wish to

scissors, then insert more pattern paper under the cut and swing the outer piece out from an imaginary pivot on the shoulder. The same is done to the second line. When pupils are happy with the flare, they should glue the pattern pieces to the additional paper underneath. They will need to redraw the shoulder and hem lines to smooth out the jagged effect created by the slashing and spreading.

To make the pattern for the facings for the neck and the front opening a line is drawn round the neck and down the centre front, 6cm away from the edge. An alternative to facings is to make a lining for the garment, like the traditional red lining of a kimono, in which case the number of pattern pieces is simply doubled.

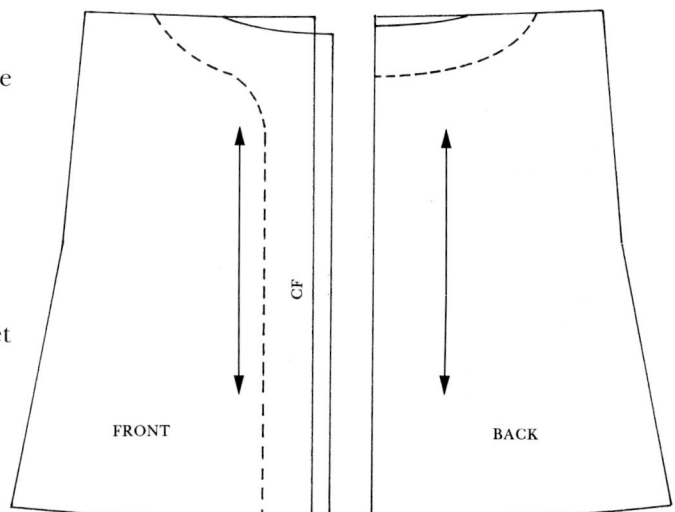

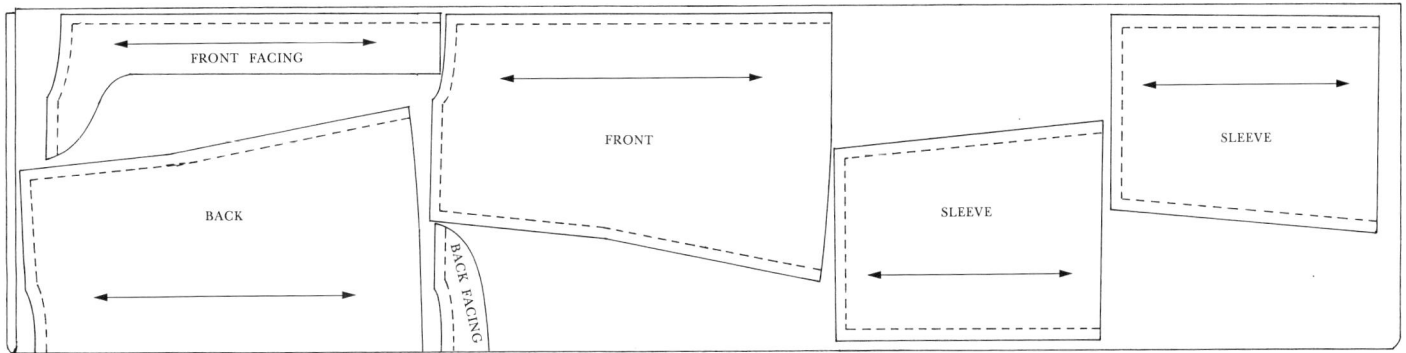

FRONT FACING

BACK

BACK FACING

FRONT

SLEEVE

SLEEVE

FOLD

The next stage is to trace off the individual pattern pieces - a pattern-cutting wheel (with sharp points) is best for this. If pupils use one they need to protect the surface underneath with strawboard or a piece of old lino. However, if the pattern paper is thin enough they should be able to see through it to trace. They must remember to make two copies of the sleeve.

Seam and hem allowances should be added to the pattern pieces that have been traced off the master copy. These are 1.5cm for seams and 4cm for the hem and the bottom of the sleeve. The width of a standard tape measure is 1.5cm so pupils could use this as a guide when marking the seam allowances. The centre back line is marked as a fold line on the back section (to be placed on the fold of material when cutting out). The pattern is now complete.

Pupils should never use a pattern they have designed themselves on a good piece of fabric without making up a trial version in cheap material such as calico or sheeting first.

When the pattern pieces have been cut out they are sewn together in the following order:

1 Sew the sleeves on to the back and front pieces at the sides. Join front and back sections along the shoulder and the top of the sleeve.

2 Sew the back and front facing pieces together at shoulders. Place them on the garment right sides together and sew along the neckline and front opening. Trim the seam allowance to 0.5cm, turn through and press.

3 Match up the underarm sleeve edge and the sides of the body. Make an L-shaped seam joining the front to the back. Reinforce with double stitching at the underarm. Trim, clip and neaten the corner under the arm.

4 Hem the sleeves and bottom of the garment.

N.B. The diagrams are not to scale.

Pupils will probably find they want to make minor adjustments. These should be marked on the trial garment pieces and the paper pattern modified accordingly. For the final garment they will need to use fabric 115cm wide. The length of fabric required is calculated by adding together twice the length of the garment, twice the length of the sleeve and their respective hem and seam allowances.

1

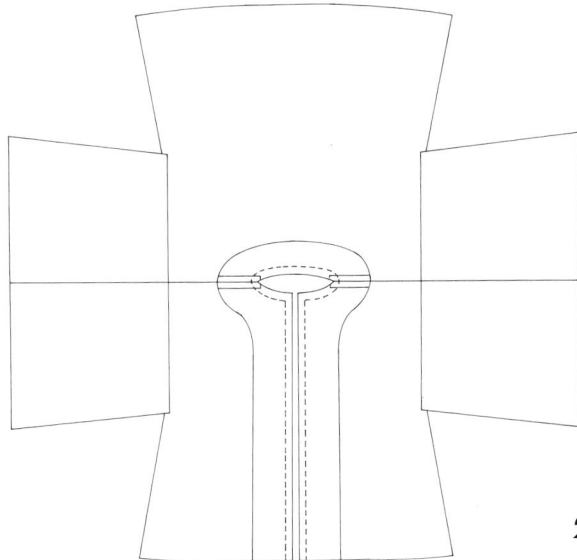

2

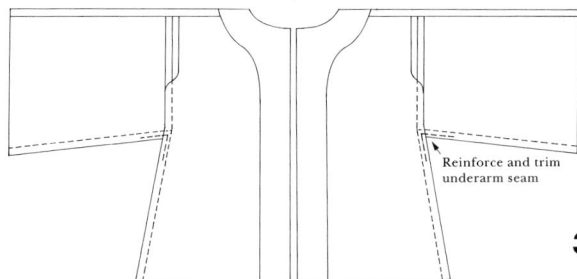

Reinforce and trim underarm seam

3

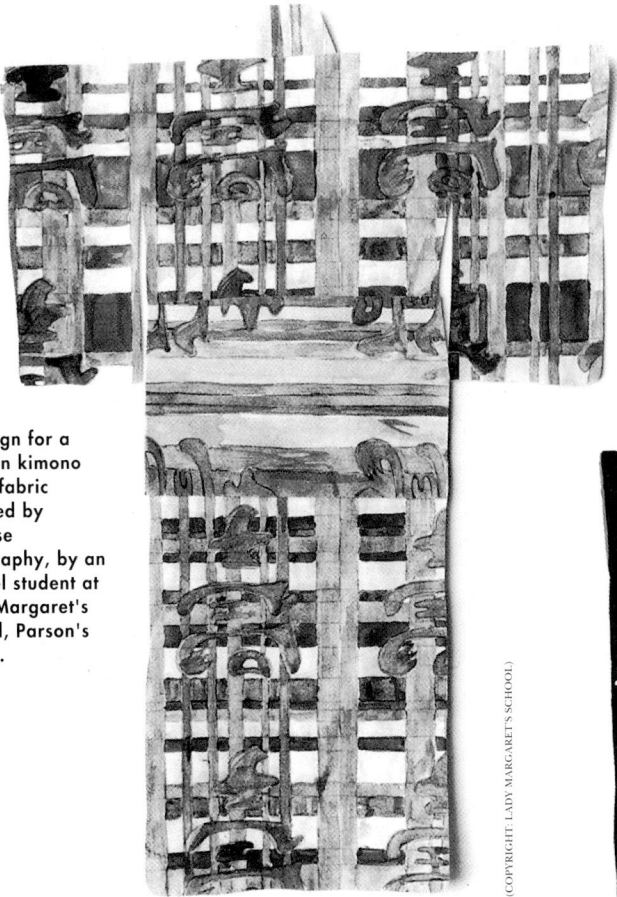

A design for a modern kimono using fabric inspired by Chinese calligraphy, by an A-level student at Lady Margaret's School, Parson's Green.

(COPYRIGHT LADY MARGARET'S SCHOOL)

Japan

Fabric to make up a Japanese kimono is purchased in a set length called a *tan*. This is about 11.7m long and about 34cm wide and is enough for one garment. Two long pieces are cut from this to make up the front and back left and the front and back right respectively. A vertical seam at the centre back joins the two sections, and further lengths are folded over and seamed to the body to form sleeves. Sleeve depths vary from garment to garment.

(FE.28-1984)

Kimono for a woman, early 19th century.

SUPPORTING INFORMATION

T-shaped garments from East Asia

Traditional clothing from the East Asian countries of Japan, China and Korea tends to conceal the form of the body. With some exceptions, it is the surface decoration of dress from Japan and China, and the striking plain colour combinations of Korean clothes that hold our attention. There are few pleats, frills or darts to be found in East Asian dress.

A crucial point about T-shaped garments from East Asia is that the cut is closely related to the loom width of the fabric used. Kimonos from Japan, for example, are made of narrow pieces of fabric sewn together with the minimum of cutting. Nowadays the standard width for the fabric used to make kimonos is about 34cm. Chinese robes use a wider width of fabric, which is shaped to form one half of the main body and the upper part of the sleeve. A typical Chinese loom width for a nineteenth-century man's dragon robe was around 60cm. Korean loom widths vary considerably but tend to be narrow.

East Asian garments generally open down the front. They are put on like a coat. In the past, because there was no need to pull the garment over the head, elaborate hairstyles and a range of hats were adopted by both men and women.

There is no seam across the shoulders, a feature common to other East Asian clothes. The edges around the neck and front opening are bound with a straight fold of material and this completes the distinctive T-shape garment.

The kimono, literally 'the thing worn', is the classic garment for both men and women. Traditionally, kimonos were worn layer upon layer. The number of layers related to the importance of the wearer; in the most extreme cases so many would be worn that the wearer could scarcely move. In reality, most women's kimonos are more intricate in structure than just described, having additional material on each side of the front opening and an extra neckband. Outer kimonos for formal wear often have an interlining and a lining. Traditionally, this lining was orangey-red in colour and curved up around the hemline so that it was visible on the outside.

This plain hem was wadded and served to weigh down the skirt so that it trailed elegantly. All kimonos are fastened with a sash called an *obi* which fits comfortably round the waist and under the hanging sleeves. The sleeves are not completely joined to the body at the armholes for this purpose.

Korea

The traditional Korean coat for a man has essentially the same cut as the Japanese kimono. It looks rather different, however, because it has additional front sections as well as tapering side extensions. This gives the Korean garment a flared shape. It is loosely fastened to the right with two long ties of matching fabric permanently sewn to the body of the garment. Inside there is a left-fastening tie. Extra cloth is also added to make the sleeves longer, and formal garments have contrasting edgings. For court robes, a closely pleated panel is sewn to the back and front skirt section and a straight red coat is worn over the top.

Korean clothes are often made from silk gauze or ramie, a fabric made from plant fibre. It is easy to mistake the main seams for the small patches often added to reinforce the delicate and transparent fabric.

Korean court robe, Choson dynasty, 1880-1910.

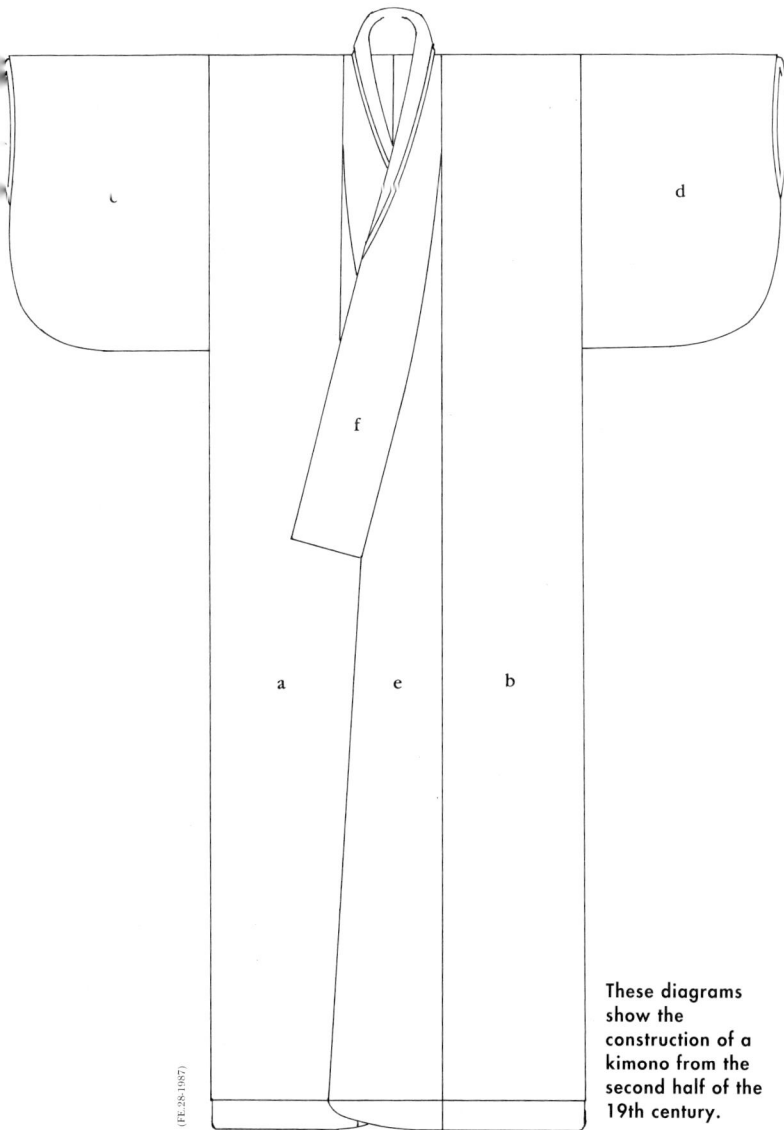

These diagrams show the construction of a kimono from the second half of the 19th century.

(This diagram is not to scale)

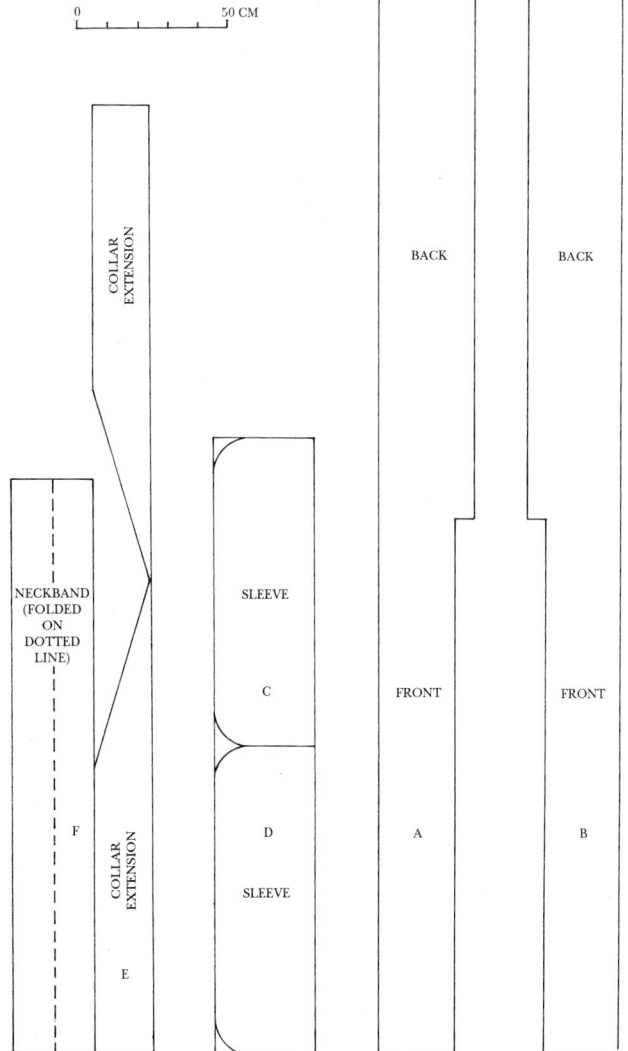

0   50 CM

COLLAR EXTENSION
NECKBAND (FOLDED ON DOTTED LINE)
COLLAR EXTENSION
SLEEVE C
SLEEVE D
BACK
BACK
FRONT A
FRONT B
F
E

China

Historic Chinese garments share some of the characteristics of those from Japan and Korea but the outline is generally more flared and the sleeves are not so deep. This silhouette was not always the norm in China. It became prevalent when the Manchus ruled the empire and introduced their dress styles from the late seventeenth century. Prior to that, clothes had greater bulk. It was the earlier Chinese style that influenced Korean dress and is preserved in the traditional Korean coat described previously.

The features of the later, slimmer Chinese robe that make it distinct from other East Asian garments are the method of closure and the shape of the sleeve ends. In the later Chinese style mensioned above, robes are cut with the body and sleeve in one piece.

(T.45-1952)

DIFFERENT MATERIAL BANDED WITH GOLD

D   D

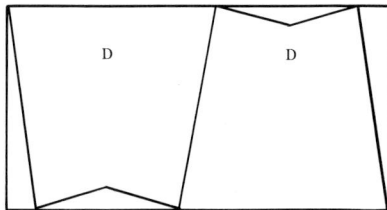

RIGHT SLEEVE   LEFT SLEEVE

Dragon robe for a woman of the imperial family, 1770-1820, Qing dynasty.

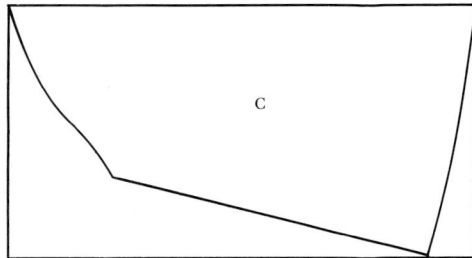

C

SIDE FASTENING FLAP

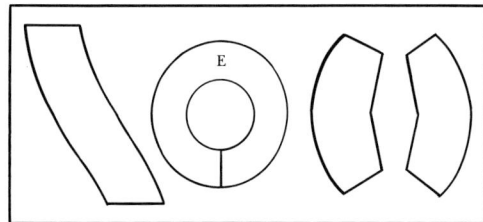

E

DIFFERENT MATERIAL

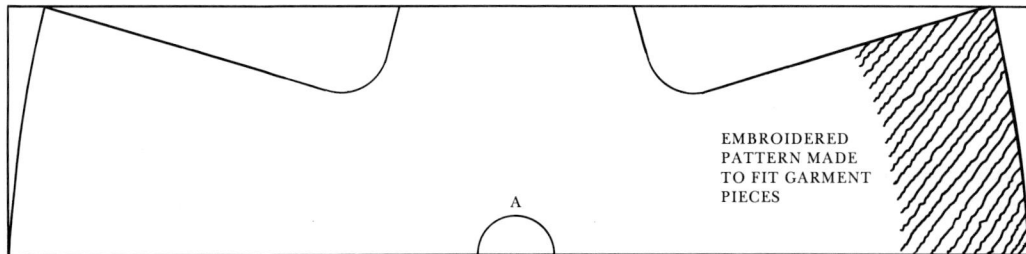

CURVED BAND   NECK BAND   HORSEHOOF CUFFS

EMBROIDERED PATTERN MADE TO FIT GARMENT PIECES

A

MAIN SECTION LEFT

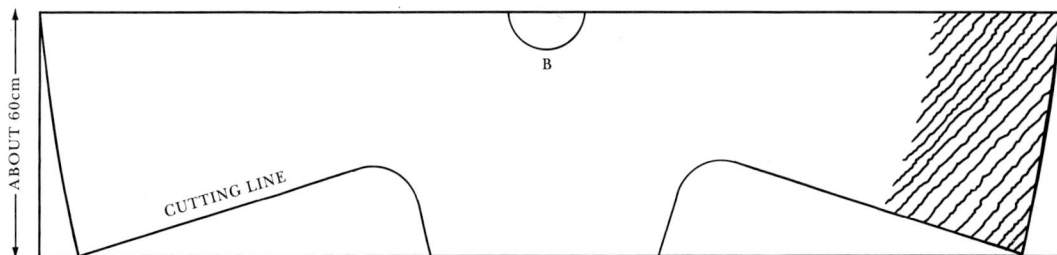

B

ABOUT 60cm

CUTTING LINE

MAIN SECTION RIGHT

ABOUT 280cm

Typical layout of pattern pieces for an early 19th-century dragon robe.

These integral upper sleeves reach to elbow level; to make them full length additional fabric is joined on. In the case of dragon-patterned official robes, which were worn by a broad sector of the male population, the lower sleeves are in a contrasting plain dark material and are sometimes crimped or banded with gold. The sleeves end in outward-curving 'horsehoof' cuffs which match the collar band.

A Chinese robe closes securely right across the front. This is achieved by using an extra length of cloth which is seamed vertically down the centre to form a complete overlap. At the top this overlap curves down and is edged with a band that is a continuation of the neck binding. The robe is fastened at the neck, along the band and down the right side with button and loop closures.

In China, garments for both men and women were generally tailored the same way. Women sometimes sported exaggerated horsehoof cuffs but usually their cuffs were straight and the sleeves looser. They wore their robes a little longer than men although they never swept the ground. Narrow woven ribbons and bias-cut embroidered bands were applied all round the edges of women's dresses.

PROJECT: SKIRTS

Activity: to design and make a skirt stylistically similar to a skirt in the Dress Collection.

Knowledge and understanding: the cut and construction of twentieth-century dress, in particular the differences between cutting on the drape and on the flat, and between using fabric on the straight and on the bias.

Galleries used: the Dress Collection

Before the visit

Discuss the differences between cutting from flat patterns and 'on the drape' with pupils using the information on the cut and construction of modern European fashion to help you. If a pattern is developed as a flat pattern from stage one then standard pattern blocks (for a bodice, skirt, sleeves and so on) can be used. The designer modifies these and often makes up a trial version in calico. Alterations are made to this (maybe involving further trial versions) and then the final pattern is cut. When cutting on the drape the designer usually develops a pattern after draping, pinning and cutting fabric on a model or dummy. Sometimes the designer works with the actual fabric for the final garment on

the dummy. In this case it is simply sewn together when the designer is happy with the design.

Discuss also how cutting on the bias or on the straight can affect the appearance of a garment. If possible look at some actual examples to demonstrate the contrast. You could arrange fabric on a mannequin to show how the direction of the grain influences the way it hangs. If you hold a piece of cloth so that the selvedges are vertical then it is hanging on the straight. Straight grain lines are marked on commercial paper patterns. These must be placed parallel to the selvedge when cutting the pieces out. If you turn a piece of cloth so that the selvedges are at a 45 degree angle to the ground then it is hanging on the bias. What is known as the true bias line is always at 45 degrees from the straight grain. Bias-cutting can be used to make the garment cling to the body as fabric cut on the bias is more elastic than that cut on the straight. Get pupils to try pulling a piece of fabric while holding it on the straight and on the bias to demonstrate this. Clothes that flow or skim across the body can also be created by cutting fabric on the bias.

At the Museum

Get pupils to look at twentieth-century skirts, both separate garments and the skirts of dresses. Point out examples of skirts cut from flat patterns and 'on the drape' and then ask pupils if they can find some more. Discuss how fit or fullness is achieved (pleats, gores etc.). Ask pupils to do drawings of one or two skirts they like, paying particular attention to shape, seams, vents, gores and fastenings. They should also note the fabric used and whether it is cut on the bias or on the straight.

Back at school

Ask your pupils to select a commercial pattern that has some of the stylistic features of one of the skirts they looked at in the Museum. Pupils could adapt the pattern by cutting it or inserting extra pattern paper as necessary. An initial 'toile' (a trial version of a garment, traditionally made of calico) should be made up in a cheap fabric like sheeting, and the pattern modified as necessary. The final design can then be made up in a suitable fabric.

SUPPORTING INFORMATION

Cut and construction of modern European fashion

There are two main methods of cutting dress -

'on the flat' and 'on the drape'. It is sometimes difficult to decide which method was used to cut clothes made in the past. Some of the more recent fashions displayed in the Dress Collection were cut from flat patterns and garment-makers at all levels, from couturiers to mass manufacturers, continue to employ this standard method. Home dressmakers are familiar with the simplest type of cutting on the flat. Using ready-made patterns, the paper pieces are placed on the fabric and cut around before sewing up.

Throughout the twentieth century numerous technical books have been published on pattern-making, garment-cutting, drafting, dressmaking and tailoring. In the rarefied world of high fashion each leading designer had his or her own distinctive method of working.

wastage of valuable material, others use cheaper lengths of muslin or calico to create a toile by draping, pleating, folding, gathering and assembling (with the aid of pins and tacking stitches) on to a figure. The construction elements such as grain of the fabric, seams, darts and turnings are marked on the cotton before the prototype is unpicked. A pattern is then taken from it and used to cut the final material on the flat.

Blouse by Digby Morton for the wartime Utility range, 1942. It was designed for mass production and a flat pattern was used. The buttons are a stylized version of the Utility symbol, CC41, which stands for Civilian Clothing 1941.

(T.45 TO B-1942)

The simple bright red Utility shirtwaister day dress in Case 49 was made for the British Board of Trade in 1942 and was probably designed by Edward Molyneux. It is a good example of cutting from a flat pattern. To boost morale and save precious commodities, the innovative Utility scheme commissioned leading British designers to provide patterns for coats, suits, blouses and dresses which were then made available to mass manufacturers. It is probable that the superbly tailored 'Chesterfield' suit of 1954 by Digby Morton (Case 50) was also developed 'on the flat'.

Many couturiers prefer the costlier 'on the drape' process and the most confident and highly skilled of them work directly with expensive fabrics, creating a garment on a dressmaker's dummy or a human body. To avoid possible

(T.31-1960)

Evening dress cut on the drape, Lucile, 1912-13.

Notable twentieth-century couturiers who favoured cutting on the drape include Lucile (Lady Duff Gordon), Madame Grès and Madeleine Vionnet. The striking evening dress of 1912-13 by Lucile (Case 43) and the white jersey evening dress by Madame Grès (Case 58) are two excellent examples of creating on the drape. The art of creating on the drape is particularly suitable for evening wear, though it is not exclusive to this area of fashion.

Fashion sketch with fabric samples attached, by Jean Muir, 1975.

fabrics, each garment in the collection is carefully sketched. The sketches, often sporting tiny fabric and trimming samples, are sometimes coloured and frequently include brief descriptions of the most important design features.

When the head designer is fully satisfied with a finished drawing of a garment it has to be made a reality. Designer and pattern cutter join forces to translate the original sketch (using precise measurements) into a calico toile. This is assembled with tacking stitches and tried on a dressmaker's dummy or a house model for careful adjustments before the calico pattern pieces are copied in heavy paper or card. From this master, in the ready-to-wear sector, the pattern is graded - translated into the various standard measurements (UK sizes 8-16) and the final flat patterns made. Clients who are wealthy enough to patronise couturiers have their clothes made to measure. A series of personal fittings ensures that they fit to perfection.

Until the outbreak of the Second World War expensive clothes were mainly hand-sewn. However, today, even at the top of the market, machine sewing dominates with some hand-stitched finishing of hems, buttonholes and fastenings.

Madeleine Vionnet's working method is noteworthy. Avoiding any preliminary sketches, she made scaled-down toiles on artist's wooden lay figures that were about 75cm high. Only when a toile satisfied Vionnet was it scaled up to full proportions.

There are several basic stages in the evolution of a garment, although every designer has an individual approach and adopts a slightly different route. The process usually starts with the selection of fabric. This choice is absolutely crucial as the type of material, its weight, pattern, colour, decoration and feel dictate the nature of a garment. Christian Dior said, 'many a dress of mine is born of the fabric alone'.

After producing the initial rough drawings showing things like colour schemes and possible

These roses on a 1987 wedding coat by John Galliano were created by hand.

FASHION PLATES AND MAGAZINES

At the end of the eighteenth century a new publishing industry arose, specifically geared to producing prints as a practical guide to current fashions. For the first time pictures were not merely illustrations, but were specifically intended to encourage the consumers themselves to wear similar clothes, or to dream about doing so.

A project based on fashion plates will give pupils the opportunity to think about how fashion is portrayed. They will need to consider the style of both clothes and fashion plates from a particular period in the past.

Fashion plate from *Le Follet*, second half of the 19th century.

LE FOLLET
(E.2438-1888)

PROJECT:
FASHION MAGAZINE SPREAD

Activity: to design a modern garment inspired by styles of a specific period from between the late eighteenth century to the 1920s; to depict the garment in a magazine spread using an appropriate graphic style based on traditional fashion plates from the relevant period.

Knowledge and understanding: dress and fashion plates from the late eighteenth century to the 1920s; the chronological development of styles during that period.

Galleries used: the Dress Collection.

Before the visit
Look at fashion spreads in some contemporary magazines with your class. Questions like these will help pupils to analyse them. What garments are shown? Who are they for? Are they cheap or expensive? Are they sensible or extravagant? What sort of figures do the models have? What mood has been created? What is the relationship of text to image?

Contemporary fashion photographs and illustrations often seem more concerned with mood and atmosphere than with presenting a clear picture of the clothes. In addition many

tricks of the trade are used, such as pinning clothes out of shot of the camera to make them hang better. Frequently the caption identifies items that are not even visible in the photograph. If you can get some examples of the drawn illustrations that are still used occasionally ask pupils why they think they were used in preference to photographs. You could also contrast fashion magazines and newspapers with mail order catalogues, which have a very different approach. Which is more likely to make you want to buy the clothes?

At the Museum
Start off by discussing some of the period fashion plates on display in the Dress Collection with your pupils. There are examples from the late eighteenth century to the 1920s. Ask pupils to look at the style of drawing (detailed, realistic, stylized, etc.), the setting for the clothes and the sort of people who are wearing them. How do they compare with the magazines and catalogues they looked at before the visit?

Each pupil now needs to make drawings and notes of at least two garments from a particular period from the late eighteenth century to 1930. They will gain more as a group if they choose different periods. Bear in mind that the closer fashion gets to the present, the faster it changes. If pupils are to develop a sense of period style, the time-span each works from should be chosen with care. For example, dress between 1790 and 1830 has a high degree of stylistic consistency, whereas between 1810 and 1850 styles changed greatly. This is something you might think about on a preparatory visit. You may find the chronology in this book helpful.

As well as drawing clothes from their period, pupils should look closely at relevant fashion plates and make sketches and notes to remind themselves of the style of illustration.

Back at school

Pupils should design a contemporary garment inspired by the styles they observed at the Museum. Final fashion magazine spreads will be prepared in appropriate media depending on your interests and the facilities you have available. Watercolour, pen and ink, etching, screen-printing and lino-printing are all possibilities. Text could be generated on a computer and the class might like to put all their work together in magazine format.

SUPPORTING INFORMATION

Fashion magazines and plates from the late eighteenth century to the 1930s

The development of fashion magazines reflects the spirit of the late eighteenth century. In earlier times only a rich few could be fashionably dressed and these were often members of royal courts. Louis XIV of France is usually credited with fostering the modern concept of swift-changing fashion. In the 1680s his glittering entourage at Versailles had little to do, so they competed with one another in dressing to impress, with new outfits for each season. This explains the beginning of the French dominance of fashion, as luxury trades grew up round the court to provide for this lucrative market. The search for novelty became the pattern for the rest of Europe.

As a result of ruthless colonial expansion in places like India in the eighteenth century and the wealth produced by the technological developments of the industrial revolution, more of the population of northern Europe could afford to be fashionably dressed. As elaborately decorated silks, which had been prohibitively expensive, fell from fashion, damasks and brocades gave way to plainer and cheaper textiles, including printed cottons. By 1800, even plain white cotton was worn by women of all social classes.

A greater number of people now wanted to know what was fashionable in London and Paris, especially if they lived far away from the capital cities. Thus the fashion plates published in the late eighteenth century in such series as the *Cabinet des modes* in France, and later in the *Gallery of fashion* and *La belle assemblée* in England, were eagerly studied and imitated. Speed of production was essential, so etching and aquatint, combined with simple hand-colouring were used by the printmakers in preference to the more expensive and slower processes of engraving or mezzotint. The prints could be shown to a local dressmaker, who would produce versions of Parisian or London dresses without venturing out of the depths of the country or the more distant industrial towns. Fashionable ideas could reach wherever the magazines could be sent.

These early prints have great elegance and charm, partly because of the simplified classical shapes of the dresses, but also because of the confident way in which the often anonymous artists composed and drew the plates. Niklaus von Heideloff, who had moved to England during the French Revolution was particularly skilled in producing attractive and plausible groupings and settings in the plates for his *Gallery of fashion*.

'Watering place, morning dress', from *Gallery of fashion*, Vol. II, Niklaus von Heideloff, 1795.

(L.254-1943)

Some fashion plates verged on caricature and portrayed eccentric behaviour as well as dress. For example, in France, Horace Vernet drew a series entitled *Les incroyables et merveilleuses* (c.1815) which depicted the extremes of contemporary fashion to comic effect.

Plate 14 from a set entitled *Les costumes d'incroyables et merveilleuses* by Horace Vernet, c.1815.

The best-known early nineteenth-century arts periodical is Ackermann's *Repository of art* which contained not only densely coloured fashion plates but also other illustrations of high fashion objects. Rudolf Ackermann judged that good-quality colour illustrations would sell goods, particularly those stocked in his shop, also called the 'Repository of Art'. His work was imitated by many, and the number of series of fashion plates available increased, but their quality progressively declined under the sheer pressure of rapid demand. Improvements in printmaking and distribution enlarged the number of magazines and the size of print runs, but an increasingly uniform look to the pictures becomes more evident towards the end of the nineteenth century when images derived from photographs of posed models were used as the basis of the pictures.

In France the couturier Paul Poiret reacted against this standardization by employing skilled painters and illustrators such as Paul Iribe (for *Les robes de Paul Poiret* of 1908) and Georges Lepape (for *Les choses de Paul Poiret* of 1911) to publicize his styles. Their work was reproduced with the highest quality of stencilled hand-colouring and issued in expensive limited editions without captions, deliberately aiming at a sophisticated audience. You can see two plates by Georges Lepape next to Case 43. Poiret had many imitators, some of whom used the same artists he had discovered.

The painterly quality of work by such artists as Raoul Dufy and Georges Barbier makes the 1920s the high point in twentieth-century fashion plates. By the end of the 1930s photography was steadily encroaching upon and even replacing the work of artists, until it became the principal way of disseminating fashion ideas in the modern world. Poiret himself had helped to initiate this trend when, as early as 1911, he commissioned the photographer Edward Steichen to photograph his garments to be reproduced in colour in the magazine *Art et decoration*.

There is a range of fashion plates on display in the Dress Collection. They are near the entrance to Gallery 21, Europe 1500 to 1600.

Three mantles designed by Paul Poiret and drawn by Paul Iribe, from *Les robes de Paul Poiret*, 1908.

THE ARCHIVE OF ART AND DESIGN

The Archive of Art and Design is a section of the Victoria and Albert Museum's National Art Library. It is housed in a separate building, near Olympia.

Among other things, it holds archival resources that complement items in the V&A's Dress Collection from the late nineteenth and twentieth centuries.

The individual archive groups consist of records created and accumulated by individuals or institutions in the course of their working or collecting life, which are thought worthy of preservation. Because of the nature of the material, the Archive is normally more appropriate for A-level than GCSE students. Pupils will need to spend at least half a day at the Archive to make a visit worthwhile.

The archive groups that relate to dress are very varied. They include groups of photographs, sketches, paper patterns, ledgers, catalogues, scrapbooks and some magazines.

Some archive groups support the Dress Collection very directly while others provide a wider and more varied view of the fashion world. A full list of dress-related archive groups is available from the Education Department.

PLANNING TO USE THE ARCHIVE

To use the Archive an appointment must be made directly with the staff there. For details of how to do this see 'Arranging a visit'. It is essential that you make a preliminary visit before bringing your pupils. This will enable you to select material and check that it will be appropriate for the needs and abilities of your pupils. A common frustration when using archives is that a lot of time can be spent sifting through material before something useful is found. Make sure you allow for this when deciding how much time to spend on a preliminary visit – a full day would not be inappropriate. At the end of the preliminary visit you can book a half-day session with the Archive for a group of up to 20 pupils. You will need to supply a list of the pupils' names for the Archive's records. Individual pupils can use the Archive without having attended a group session, but you will still need to make a preliminary visit yourself so that you are aware of the sort of material they will be presented with.

Lead pencil only may be used at the Archive, photocopying and tracing are not permitted, and only photography without flash for reference purposes is allowed. This is because pupils are handling original artefacts. The Rules of the Reading Room are available for consultation at the Archive.

Pupils should be encouraged to make as full a record as possible of relevant aspects of the material they are looking at.

Here are some useful questions to bear in mind when looking at individual archive groups at the Archive of Art and Design:

- Approximately how many individual items are there?

- Do they look old or new? If they look old, what signs of wear are there?

- Were they hand-written or -drawn, or printed? Unique or mass-produced?

- Is there anything obviously missing (for example, dates in a chronological sequence, pages torn out of note-books, etc.)?

- Who used the material in the archive group?

- What for?

- Who did the archive group belong to before being collected by the Archive of Art and Design?

- What factual information does the archive group give you?

- What more general points can you deduce from it?

- Why do you think the archive group was valuable to the original owner (sentimental value, aesthetic value, monetary value, business records, records of designs, etc.)?

- Why do you think the archive group has survived?

Unlike textbooks, or even galleries in a museum, archives present unmediated primary source material. It is therefore especially important that pupils have done sufficient preparation in the classroom or library to enable them to extract relevant information. Archives are, by their nature, partial and selective. Pupils will need background knowledge so that they have a sense of the significance of what they are looking at.

Page from a Lilley & Skinner shoe catalogue, late 1920s.

It is important to realize that the kind of questions that can be answered by archival material are not always easy to predict in advance. Pupils should have some idea about what they want to find out but should be prepared to use the strengths of the material they are presented with.

Using the Archive of Art and Design will help develop valuable research skills. Make sure pupils keep precise references of the archive groups they look at. Each archive group has a museum reference number and there are often additional identifying numbers for items within an archive group. Suggest to pupils that they record everything they look at even if they find it is not very useful. If an archive group is not useful they should make a note of why not. That way they demonstrate that they are capable of discriminating between relevant and irrelevant information.

The projects below are described in detail to give you examples of the kind of work it is possible to do using the Archive of Art and Design. They make use of archive groups that are both readily accessible to A-level pupils and tie in well with the displays in the Dress Collection. They may also be appropriate to some GCSE groups. Shoes, accessories and knitwear are among other dress topics that can be supported by the Archive.

PROJECT: TEA GOWNS

Activity: to design a light, romantic party dress that is a modern interpretation of the tea gown.

Knowledge and understanding: the factors that characterized tea gowns and distinguished them from other types of special occasion wear; how the style of tea gowns by the House of Worth developed in the period 1899 to 1914.

Galleries used: the Dress Collection; the Archive of Art and Design.

Before the visit

Discuss with pupils the idea of clothes for special occasions. Maybe some of them could bring in examples of clothes that they would only wear on special occasions (a party outfit or a bridesmaid's dress, for example). What is it that makes these clothes different to the ones they wear every day?

Ask pupils how many times they change their clothes in a day. In the past wealthy people changed their clothes far more frequently than we do today. At the turn of the century well-to-do women had different outfits for different times of the day as well as for different activities. The tea gown was a type of loose-fitting dress normally worn by women when entertaining friends at afternoon tea. It had a fairly high neck and was typically a light and frothy creation in a pale colour. Show pupils some pictures of tea gowns so they know what to look out for at the Archive.

At the Archive

The House of Worth was established in Paris in 1858 by the Englishman Charles Frederick Worth. He is often described as the first couturier. After his death in 1895 the House of Worth was taken over by his sons. It remained in the family until 1954 when it was bought out by Paquin, a rival couture house. Two years later the House of Worth closed. Parfum Worth continues the name.

At the Archive pupils will be looking at House of Worth tea gowns and other special occasion wear from 1899 to 1914. This period was the heyday of the tea gown. The clothes pupils will be looking at were designed by Worth's son, Jean-Philippe Worth.

The Archive of Art and Design houses two major House of Worth archive groups (museum reference numbers AAD.4-1990 and AAD.1-1982) both of which can be used for this project. Both consist primarily of photographs in albums, although the former also contains some loose photographs. The albums, of which there are about 100, were produced by the couture house as a record of each season's fashions. Frequently, there are two photographs of each item from different angles, or the gown is positioned in front of a mirror so that the back is visible. As the groups are so large, precise references for individual items are given below.

Pupils should use the Worth albums to see how the style of the tea gown developed from the end of the nineteenth century to the First World War. There are examples of tea gowns in all the albums of special occasion wear from this period. They are referred to as 'robe de thé' in the earlier albums and 'tea gown' in the later

Page from a
Worth album
showing a ball
gown, 1913-14.

(AAD.1/61-1982)

ones. The changing frequency with which they occur gives an indication of their rise and fall amongst the wealthy, fashionable women who were Worth's clients. Pupils might also compare the tea gowns to other types of special occasion wear in the same albums, such as 'deshabillé' gowns (another type of loose, informal dress, cut lower at the neck than a tea gown) and ball gowns.

On each page of the album there are brief notes in French on fabrics and colours which give valuable additional information. You do not need to have an extensive knowledge of French to translate most of these notes. Examples of words you may find are 'bleu' and 'chiffon'. French-language dictionaries are available in the reading room. The references for the relevant albums are AAD.1/41-1982 to AAD.1/61-1982. As each one contains about 100 photographs it is a good idea to select three or four albums only initially. Pick ones that are well spaced out chronologically.

In the other Worth archive group are two loose photographs of a model wearing a tea gown. These are useful because they show how the gown would have looked when worn. The references for the photographs are: AAD.4/8-1990 and AAD.4/6-1990. There are two further photographs, AAD.4/11-1990 and AAD.4/12-1990, which make a good point of comparison to the tea gown. They show an evening dress that is very similar in style to a tea gown.

At the Museum

In the Dress Collection get pupils to look at the Worth tea gown in Case 42. It is better to visit the Museum after the Archive so that pupils will be able to make detailed observations about the gown on display, placing it in the context of the other Worth tea gowns they have looked at. It can also be compared to other types of special occasion dress by Worth and others in adjacent cases.

Pupils will have the opportunity to make drawings of the tea gown in colour (which they will have been unable to do at the Archive). They could also do some sketches of details such as trimmings and examine how the tea gown is constructed, looking particularly at the use of layers of fabric and the degree to which it is fitted to the body shape.

Back at school

You might want to discuss with pupils the relative usefulness of the information they obtained from the Dress Collection and the Archive. What were the strengths and weaknesses of each as a resource? The final stage of the project is for pupils to do their own original designs for a reinterpretation of the tea gown. They should think about the kind of fabrics it might be made up in and attach some suitable samples.

PROJECT:

HATS AND HAIR ACCESSORIES

Activity: to design a hat or hair accessory to go with an outfit made between 1890 and 1910.

Knowledge and understanding: the importance of hats and hairstyles to an overall fashion look; knowledge of hats, hairstyles and hair accessories from 1890 to 1910.

Galleries used: the Dress Collection; the Archive of Art and Design.

Before the visit

Think about how important the head is to an overall look. Pupils could explore this by sticking new heads cut from magazines on to models in advertisements or fashion spreads. If they stick them on with Blutak then they can compare the effect of different heads. Discuss the features that make the original head go with the clothes. How does a new head change the appearance of the outfit?

The design brief for the project is:
The Textiles and Dress Department at the V&A

Page from an album of hairstyles by Jean Stehr, 1895.

(AAD.11-1983)

hairstyles featuring a variety of hats and ornaments. This London-based hairdressing company appears to have specialized in elaborate and fanciful coiffures – exactly the sort of thing that, for a special occasion, might have been worn with the high fashion clothes in the Dress Collection. Pupils should make drawings of some of the hairstyles, recording particularly carefully any hats, hairpins, combs or other hair ornaments.

At the Museum

All the hairstyles on the mannequins in the Dress Collection are historically accurate and so can usefully be compared to those in the Jean Stehr archive group. Original or replica hats and hair ornaments are often part of each outfit and there are originals on display in separate cases. The holdings from the period 1890 to 1910 complement the Jean Stehr material.

Ask pupils to choose an outfit for which they are going to design a hat or hair accessory and record it carefully, including the head and hairstyle. They should also sketch some original hats or hair ornaments from the relevant period.

Back at school

The task back at school is for pupils to design an alternative hair accessory and/or hat to go with the outfit they chose. It should be shown worn with an appropriate hairstyle. Their design will incorporate elements from their drawings at the Museum and the Archive and could be accompanied by a design rationale that refers to the characteristics of hats and hairstyles of the period.

needs to take some of the turn-of-the-century hats and hair accessories off display to be cleaned and repaired. They will have to be replaced with replicas in correct period style. The task for pupils is to design and make a hat or hair accessory to go with an outfit from 1890 to 1910.

At the Archive

The Jean Stehr archive group (AAD.11-1983) consists of two albums of drawn illustrations of

Assorted hair ornaments: comb, last quarter of the 19th century; headband, Schiaparelli, 1938; hatpins, English 1953-55.

(T.263-1958, T.414-1974, T.66-1983)

PROJECT:
FASHIONS OF THE 1960S, '70S AND '80S

Activity: to compile a report on the fashions of the 1960s, '70s or '80s for use by theatre, film and television costume designers.

Possible extension: to design a fabric inspired by the patterns and colours from one of these decades.

Knowledge and understanding: the differences between mass-market fashion and high fashion in the 1960s, '70s and '80s as represented in a range of sources; an awareness of fashion forecasting agencies as a means of distilling the essence of high fashion trends for use in mass-production.

Galleries used: the Dress Collection; the Archive of Art and Design.

Before the visit

People who design costumes for theatre, film and television need easy-to-use guides to the fashions of the past. The brief for your pupils is to imagine they are preparing a guide to the fashions of the 1960s, '70s or '80s for a costume designer to use.

Ask pupils to bring in family photographs to help them build up a picture of what ordinary people were wearing during these periods. Oral history would provide another fruitful starting-point. Pupils could ask parents, grandparents and friends of the family about what they used to wear when they were younger. They might tape-record interviews or devise a questionnaire. Second-hand clothes shops and jumble sales may have real examples that could be purchased cheaply. Pupils could then make a display of the photographs and garments with appropriate captions.

Books on the history of fashion and monographs on individual designers will give pupils information about high fashion. Local libraries often keep back copies of up-market fashion magazines such as *Vogue*, which are good sources of information about high fashion and the more expensive type of ready-to-wear clothes. As a result of their research pupils should decide which decade they would like to research further.

At the Archive

Presage is a French company that produced seasonal brochures of colours and fabric samples used by manufacturers in the design of new collections. Such forecasting agencies are influential, reducing high fashion trends and developments in fabric technology to an easily assimilable reference format.

The Presage fashion forecasts are stored in the Reading Room and arranged chronologically from 1962 to 1988. There are several volumes for each year. Each volume deals with a different aspect of fashion textiles, with the emphasis on fabrics, colours and patterns. For example, there is usually one on printed fabrics and one on colour ranges and combinations.

You might want to go through a sample year as a group so your pupils get the feeling for the kind of information the forecasts provide. They can then select volumes from the decade they have chosen to study. They might find it helpful to record information in the form of a visual chart of key colour combinations, fabrics and patterns from their decade. They should also note how the information is presented (pull-out charts, swatches, colour circles, etc.) as they could use some of the formats for their own reports.

At the Museum

Pupils should consider the extent to which the high fashion garments in the Dress Collection from the 1960s, '70s or '80s anticipate the Presage fashion forecasts, and contrast the use of colour and fabrics by top designers with mass-market fashions of the period. Get pupils to look with this in mind and make notes of their observations. They could also do sketches of individual garments.

Back at school

Pupils should compile their findings into a format that makes it easy to see the key features of the decade they have chosen. A good textiles project back at school would be to design a patterned fabric inspired by the 1960s, '70s or '80s using an appropriate colourway and motifs.

An extension might be to ask pupils to think about contemporary fashions. What colours, fabrics, shapes and styles are currently 'in'? Get them to do a survey of several high street stores and compile their results into an illustrated table.

Page from Presage fashion forecast - 'tissés/lainages', 1983.

(UNREGISTERED. ARCHIVE OF ART & DESIGN)

AÉRIENS LES VOILES DE COTON

COLORÉS, LES COTONS IMPRIMÉS

241
285
286
202
215
200
318
201
244
203

CHRONOLOGY

Gown with a standing
semi-circular collar,
early 17th century.

(189-1900)

Doublet, breeches and
cloak, c.1630.

(T.58 TO B-1910)

Mantua, c.1720.

(T.136, T.137 AND T.138-1967)

Dress suit, late 1720s o
early 1730s.

(T.88 TO B1978)

White muslin
evening dress
worn with a
scarf from the
first decade of
the 19th century.

(T.124-1913, 678-1893)

Double-breasted dress
coat, waistcoat and
'cossack' trousers from
the 1820s.

(T.136, T.137 AND T.138-1967)

Dress, c.1828, and large
bonnet, c.1830.

Dress, c.1842.

(T.151-1968, T.130-1962)

Dress coat and linen
trousers, late 1840s,
early 1850s.

(T.848-1974)

Double-breasted suit,
c.1904, and boater,
late 19th or early
20th century.

Summer day dress,
c.1910.

(T.159 & A-1960, T.81-1980)

Evening dress, Patou,
1925-26.

(T.465-1974)

Evening dress,
Norman Hartnell,
1933-34.

(T.198-1970)

Single-breasted suit,
1940.

(T.196-1973)

Utility suit, probably by
Victor Stiebel, 1942.

(T.717 AND A-1974)

Robe and petticoat, 1740s.

Dress coat and waistcoat, 1760s.

Robe, 'Polonaise', 1775-80.

Double-breasted morning coat and waistcoat, 1790s.

Day dress, 1873-75.

Double-breasted morning coat, 1873-75.

Evening dress, possibly a copy of a Worth original, 1894.

Robe by Liberty, late 1890s.

Dance dress, Christian Dior, 1955.

Day dress and jacket, Ungaro, 1966.

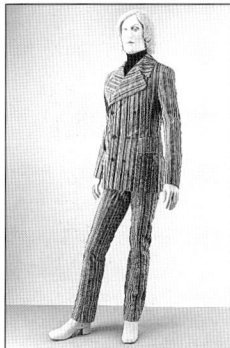

Double-breasted suit, Mr Fish, c.1968.

Evening dress and hat, Jean Muir, 1971.

Pirate outfit, Vivienne Westwood, 1980.

Single-breasted suit, Tommy Nutter, 1983.

SUPPORTING THE NATIONAL CURRICULUM AND EXAMINATION COURSES

Art

One of the key elements of the Art National Curriculum is that pupils should make links between investigating and making, and knowledge and understanding. The Art Order states that 'although the programmes of study have been set out in relation to each attainment target, there is no implication that teaching activities or learning opportunities should be designed to address them separately'. There are explicit demands that pupils should make connections between their own work and that of others.

Critical Studies involving knowledge, understanding and evaluation of the work of past and present artists, designers and craftspeople is an important part of all Art GCSE and A-level syllabuses. Similarly, for BTEC First and National Diplomas and GNVQ qualifications in Art and Design one of the core elements is the history and traditions of Art and Design. The essence of BTEC is that all the elements of the syllabus are integrated and this is made very clear in the course descriptions for the new Art and Design GNVQs. For example, in the course description for the advanced level GNVQ in Art and Design it states: 'You investigate and analyse historical and contemporary influences on the work of artists, designers and art movements, before relating them to your work'.

All the projects described in the publication suggest ways of generating practical work from

Critical Studies. Those in the chapter on the Archive of Art and Design have a greater emphasis on the Critical Studies element and look at ways of using archival sources in conjunction with the Dress Collection.

Textiles and Technology

The projects in this book require pupils to work with a range of compliant and resistant materials in addition to textiles, which is consistent with the Technology National Curriculum. The 'design and make' nature of most of the projects described, and the inclusion of the analysis of products by influential designers and manufacturers, means that they are close to the spirit of the National Curriculum recommendations.

At A-level, specialized Textiles courses generally have an option on clothing and normally require historical knowledge of the subject. The Northern Examinations and Assessment Board even goes so far as to make specific reference to the value of the V&A's collections as a key resource.

The BTEC First and National Diplomas in the areas of Design, and Fashion and Textiles demand an integrated approach. Practical work is related to students' understanding of how the design of others is affected by historical, social, economic and multicultural factors.

The projects outlined here support both BTEC and A-level syllabuses very well.

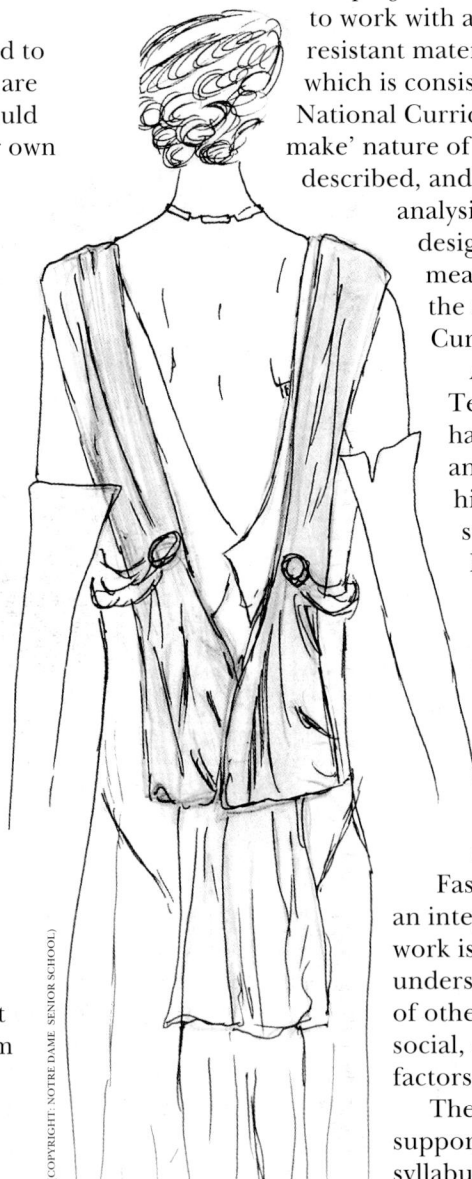

Drawing of a 1933 evening dress by Paul Poiret for Liberty & Co., GCSE student, Notre Dame Senior School, Lingfield.

(COPYRIGHT: NOTRE DAME SENIOR SCHOOL)

FURTHER READING AND RESOURCES

General books on the Dress Collection
Rothstein, N. (ed), *Four hundred years of fashion*, Victoria and Albert Museum, 1984, reprinted 1992, ISBN 1-85177-116-6. Essential guide to the Dress Collection.

Wilcox, C., Mendes, V. *Modern fashion in detail*, Victoria and Albert Museum, 1991, ISBN 1-85177-032-1. An excellent reference book featuring large, full-colour photographs of details such as seams, buttons and bows, together with line drawings of whole garments.

The changing shape of fashion
Buck, A.M. *Victorian costume and costume accessories*, Bean, R. 1984, ISBN 0-903585-17-0

Buxton, A. *Discovering nineteenth-century fashion*, Hobsons, 1989, ISBN 1-85324-161-X. This book for pupils uses items from the V&A's collections as examples. It suggests activities, research and projects for pupils to do.

Ewing, E. *Dress and undress*, Batsford, 1978, ISBN 0-7134-1629-7

Laver, J. *Costume and fashion: a concise history*, Thames & Hudson 'World of art' series, revised edition 1982, ISBN 0-500-20190-0. An invaluable and authoritative guide. Describes the development of fashion from ancient times to the twentieth century.

Wilson, E., Taylor, L. *Through the looking glass: a history of dress from 1860 to the present day*, BBC Books, 1989, ISBN 0-563-21441-4. A key work, particularly good on the social and historical context for fashion.

Historical and cross-cultural influences on twentieth-century fashion
(see also the books on non-European dress listed for Cut and construction)

de la Haye, A. *The fashion source book*, Quarto, 1988, ISBN 0- 356-15928-0. A history of leading twentieth-century couturiers and an analysis of the dress of less-wealthy sectors of society. It looks at men's, women's and children's fashion decade by decade. This book is useful because it deals with contemporary designers.

Lurie, A. *The language of clothes*, Bloomsbury, 1981, revised edition 1992, ISBN 0-7475-0821-6. A thought-provoking discussion of the things clothes say about the wearer.

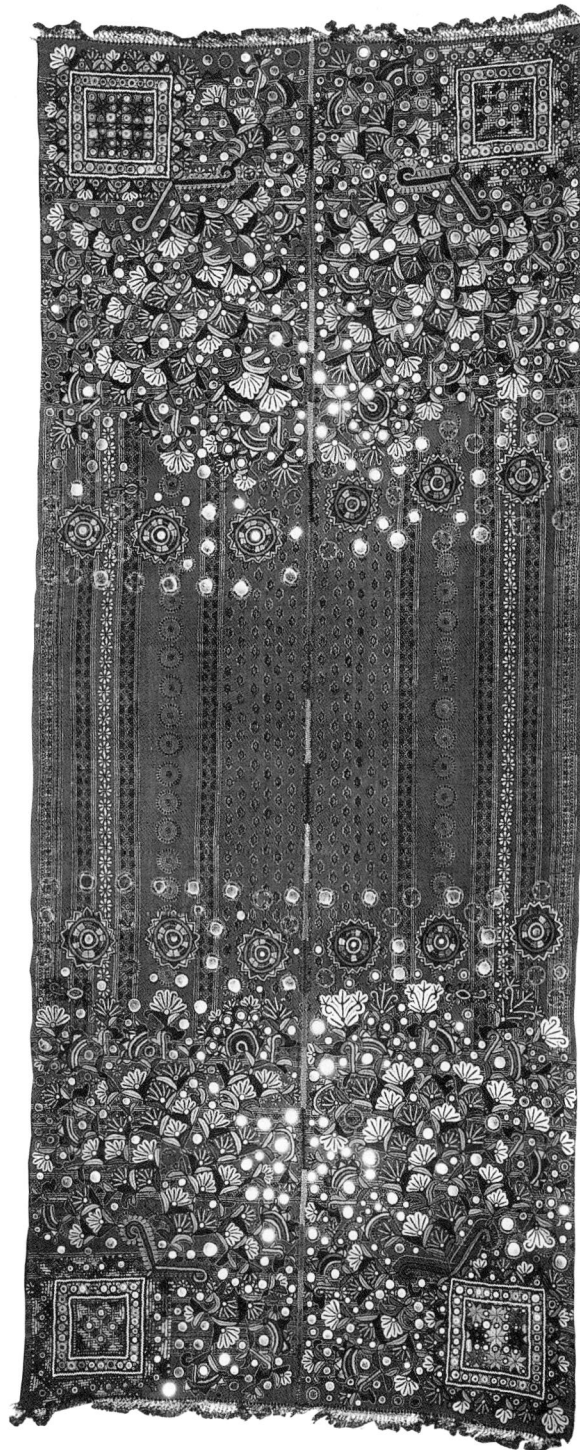

Indian embroidered shawl for a man, early 20th century.

Cut and construction
Arnold, J. *Patterns of fashion, Vols 1 and 2*, Macmillan, 1972, Vol 1 ISBN 0-333-13606-3, Vol 2 0-333-13607-1. Includes analysis of the cut and construction of items in the V&A's collection.

Crill, R., Guy, J., Murphy, V., Stronge, S., Swallow, D. *Arts of India: 1550-1900*, Victoria and Albert Museum, 1990, ISBN 1-85177-022-4

Earle, J., Faulkner, R., Wilson, V., Kerr, R., Clunas, C. *Japanese art and design*, Victoria and Albert Museum, 1986, ISBN 0-948107-65-0

Kennedy, A. *Japanese Costume*, Éditions Adam Biro, 1990, ISBN 2-87660-083-8

McKillop, B. *Korean art and design*, Victoria and Albert Museum, 1992, ISBN 1-85177-104-2
Waugh, N. *The cut of women's clothes*, Faber, 1968, ISBN 0-571-08594-6
Wilson, V. *Chinese dress*, Victoria and Albert Museum Far Eastern Series/Bamboo Books, 1989, ISBN 1-870076-14-1. A good detailed guide to Chinese dress in the V&A's collection. Gives valuable information on the history and social context of Chinese dress.

Fashion plates
Ginsburg, M. *An introduction to fashion illustration*, Victoria and Albert Museum/Compton/Pitman, 1980, ISBN 0-273-01471-4

La corbeille vivante (the living flower basket), a fashion plate from Le bon genre, 1817.

Paris.   Le Bon Genre.   N° 71.

La Corbeille Vivante.

The Archive of Art and Design
Carnegy, V. *Fashions of a decade: the 1980s*, Batsford, 1990, ISBN 0-7134-6436-4. One of a colourful, accessible series of books on each decade from the 1920s to the '90s with lots of illustrations and concise text. Gives some of the social and historical background to fashion. Each has a glossary and a reading list that includes books for young people as well as adults.
Clark, F. *Hats*, Batsford, 1982, ISBN 0-7134-3774-X
Coleman, E.A. *The opulent era: fashions of Worth, Doucet and Pingat*, Brooklyn Museum/Thames & Hudson, 1989, ISBN 0-500-01476-0
Connikie, Y. *Fashions of a decade: the 1960s*, Batsford, 1990, ISBN 0-7134-6437-2
Corson, R. *Fashions in hair*, Peter Owen, ISBN 0-7206-3283-8
Herald, J. *Fashions of a decade: the 1970s*, Batsford, 1992, ISBN 0-7134-6805-X

Booklists
Booklists on various aspects of dress are available from the Textiles and Dress Collection, Victoria and Albert Museum, Cromwell Road, South Kensington, London SW7 2RL. Please send a large SAE.

Other resources
Original fashion sketches, particularly before 1900, are held in the Prints, Drawings and Paintings Collection of the V&A. There is a microfiche register of these catalogued up to 1981: Visual catalogue of fashion and costume in the V&A.

The Museum shop has a range of postcards of European dress, including some of details. There are also postcards of Chinese, Japanese, Korean and Indian dress, and fashion plates.

Acknowledgements
We would like to thank these schools for providing feedback about how they followed up their visit to the Museum:
Aylwin School, Bermondsey, London; Buckler's Mead Community School, Yeovil, Somerset; Dunraven School, Streatham, London; Lady Margaret's School, Parson's Green, London; George Green's School, Isle of Dogs, London; Holy Cross Convent School, New Malden, Surrey; John Bunyan Upper School, Bedford, Bedfordshire; Kingswinford School, Kingswinford, West Midlands; Longford School, Feltham, Middlesex; Notre Dame Senior School, Lingfield, Surrey; Pipers Corner School, High Wycombe, Buckinghamshire; South-East Essex Sixth Form College, Benfleet, Essex; The Tiffin Girls' School, Kingston-upon-Thames, Surrey; Tolworth Girls' School, Surbiton, Surrey.

The Trustees of the Victoria and Albert Museum would like to thank the V&A Patrons for their generous support.